Wendy on . . .

Fashion
Say what you want, ladies, but you looking your best is very important to your man. . . . [D]on't be afraid to be sexy. It *does* matter how you look.

What *not* to have in the bedroom
Pictures of family, friends, and children. That unicorn you won at Six Flags when you were nineteen. Bills.

Liposuction
I'm sorry if I'm not like you—accepting yourself as you are. . . . I know I'm not perfect but plastic surgery has allowed me the freedom mentally to be me. . . . I feel sexy and I feel great.

Laugh lines
You owe it to yourself to have a big sense of humor. If you can laugh, even in the most difficult situations, your relationship will last longer.

Divorce
Keep the wedding ring.

Courage
When things go wrong and your strength is really tested, have the courage to see it through. It's easy to be courageous when everything is going right, but when things are going wrong for you, have courage—it will carry you far.

Wendy's Got the Heat

Wendy's Got the Heat

WENDY WILLIAMS

WITH KAREN HUNTER

POCKET BOOKS

New York   London   Toronto   Sydney

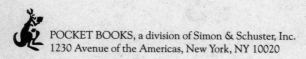 POCKET BOOKS, a division of Simon & Schuster, Inc.
1230 Avenue of the Americas, New York, NY 10020

ISBN: 0-7434-7021-4
      0-7434-7022-2 (Pbk)

First Pocket Books trade paperback edition August 2004

10 9 8 7 6 5 4 3 2 1

POCKET BOOKS and colophon are registered trademarks of
Simon & Schuster, Inc.

Manufactured in the United States of America

For information regarding special discounts for bulk purchases,
please contact Simon & Schuster Special Sales at 1-800-456-6798
or business@simonandschuster.com

To my husband and my son.
To my mom and my dad.
To my sister and my brother.
And to everyone who has ever supported my futuristic vision.

Contents

Foreword

WHEN I SAT DOWN TO WRITE *Wendy's Got the Heat*, I just wanted to write my story—the story of a simple girl from Jersey. I figured a few people would be interested—those who knew me from the radio in the tri-state area and maybe some fans from Philadelphia where I spent a few years on the air. But a *New York Times* Best Seller? It's not something I ever imagined.

The *New York Times* Best Seller's List—that was for real authors, real writers. That is the pinnacle for any book.

I got the fax on Tuesday before the list was to be published, which is on Sundays. My editor, Malaika Adero, sent over a fax that read, "You are No. 9 on the *New York Times* Best Seller's List" and she included the list.

On the list at No. 1 was *Kate Remembered*, the memoir of Katherine Hepburn who had died that year. In addition was *Seabiscuit*; Hillary Clinton's book; a book about the Kennedy clan; and there I was debuting at No. 9—the only black woman, hell, the only black *period* on the entire list.

When the list came out, E. Lynn Harris was among the first to send me flowers. He came on my show the following week to promote his book, *A Love of My Own*, which was his autobiography. On the show he said, "Wendy, we're part of an exclusive club—blacks who have made the *New York Times* Best Seller's List." What an honor. I am such a fan of E. Lynn Harris and to be even considered in the same league . . . well! It's a bit overwhelming.

And I owe it all to you people—all of you who stood in line for hours at a book signing, who bought two and three books to give to friends and family members, who supported *Wendy's Got the Heat,* and who have been supporting this simple girl from Jersey by listening to my show. I truly thank you.

The book tour officially kicked off in August—a full month earlier than expected. I had taken a month off to prepare for this book tour. I had never done anything like this, so I wanted to make sure I had the right clothes and the right attitude. I went shopping and I even got a special pen made—a pink plume with a long pink feather. I wanted to sign with all of the drama and flair that I have become known for.

But I didn't have as much time as I expected to prepare because we started getting calls while I was out. People were calling the studio and telling my replacement and my producer that the books were selling on 125th Street, Journal Square in Jersey City, New Jersey, and in parts of Brooklyn. Yes, my book was being bootlegged. That was unheard of, from what I am told. And that was the impetus to move the publishing date up a month.

And shout-outs to the bootleggers. I used to support you when you were bootlegging music. But since it has happened to me, I started hating. I realized how deep to the core that an artist must hurt. I still, however, show you love because you too helped put *Wendy's Got the Heat* in a whole other category.

My first book signing was at Virgin Mega Store in the middle of Times Square. I wore black silk party pants with ruffles and a matching silk shirt with ruffles. I felt like Miss Lena Horne, like a real celebrity when I arrived by limo. I felt like Mariah Carey, you know when she has those major album droppings and signings. And I kept thinking, "All of this for me?"

On the ride over, my biggest fear was that no one would show up. My husband, who is also my manager, had these grand visions, though. He always believed. He always knew. I didn't.

My clothes were right. My hair was right. My makeup was right. My shoes were right. I had my special pen. But I was a complete mess inside. I was a nervous wreck. I thought I would get there and it would be really embarrassing. I also thought at least I looked nice for our dinner later that evening with my agent, Ian Kleinert.

But when I arrived at the Virgin Mega Store, it was a mob scene. I was completely wrong. There was such a crowd that we ran out of books. Wyclef Jean even showed up and bought five books— one for his wife, his security, Beast, and for other family members. Shout out to Wyclef. He's a big supporter, always has been.

Everything went off without a hitch. And that set the tone for the rest of the signings throughout New York, New Jersey, and Philadelphia. Our biggest problem was keeping enough books in the stores for the crowds—from the Short Hills Mall to the Harlem Book Fair to the International House of Pancakes in

Newark, New Jersey (which I admit was the strangest place to sign books, but I love my people and I will go whether they are).

I learned that the people who listen to my radio show are some of the most wonderful and diverse people in the world—black, white, rich, poor, young, old. I met a twelve-year-old listener, who came with her thirty-six-year-old mother who also listens, and who bought a book for her sixty-year-old mother who also listens. I also learned that my book touched people in ways I could never imagine. I heard from people who told me their story is similar to mine. So many people told me they cried when they read the book and were inspired by my story. I even had people tell me that this book changed their lives.

This simple story about a girl from New Jersey changed lives. That's humbling. And I am grateful that it is now coming out in paperback so even more people can afford to experience *Wendy's Got the Heat*.

I also learned that I love writing, I love sharing stories, and this is just the beginning. Expect more advice, more personal stories, more Wendy in the future. I am even delving into writing novels—all of those stories I could never share on the air will now make their way in some form into a novel.

I have packed a lot of living in my short time on this earth and it's been my pleasure to share a piece of it with you. And if there is anything that you can related to or that can help you get through a situation you are struggling with—whether it's drug abuse or having a baby—know that you are not alone.

You will find a little bit of everything in this book. Thank you for supporting me. Enjoy!

Wendy's Got the Heat

Futuristic Vision

BITCHES AND NIGGAS EVERY DAY are practicing to do my shit. Bitches every day are eyeing this number one spot. And I'm not threatened by it at all because I know a few things. First, I didn't get here just because. I worked very hard. And, second, just like I got here, I know it can all be taken away. So I continue to work hard. I take nothing for granted.

The top radio personalities in the country are all men—Howard Stern, Don Imus, Tom Joyner and so on. I am the top woman, nationally—even before syndication. In terms of money, in terms of industry recognition and prestige, I am number one. Yes, people know Robin Quivers and perhaps Robin Quivers even makes more money than I do, but she is not in my class because she is riding the coattails of a major male jock—Howard Stern. And I'm not hating on Robin for being Ed McMahon to Howard's Johnny Carson. All I'm saying is that my show is *The Wendy Williams Experience*. I'm nobody's sidekick.

In my market, LITE-FM is usually the number one show during the afternoon drive. I'm number two. When I came back to New York to WBLS, it was number fifteen during the afternoons. In one book, which is only three months, I took them to number two. Number two for me is like being number one because LITE-FM, which plays easy-listening music like Celine Dionne, is generally the station of choice for most businesses. When you walk into a business, LITE-FM provides that background, mood music. If I walk into a business and they do have *The Wendy Williams Experience* on, I'm thinking that they are more interested in gossip than the business. I mean really. What kind of respectable business would be tuning into my show during business hours?

So I will concede the number one spot to LITE-FM. But answer me this: Who is LITE-FM's afternoon jock? I couldn't tell you.

Women ask me all the time how can they break into the business, how do they get down. How you get down? The quickest way to get down in this business as a woman is to "get down," if you know what I mean. If you are willing to compromise yourself with a program director or an owner or executive of one of these radio conglomerates that own twenty-five stations across the country, you can all but guarantee yourself a job. He might put you in Nebraska but you can bet you'll be his Nebraska chick. If you can suck a mean dick, you can become his Boston chick. Hey, I think that's the number seven market. You poke a hole in the condom and have his baby, that might land you a New York spot because now you got his secret. There are women in all professions who got their jobs that way.

But for me, I somehow knew that getting my job that way would taint everything I was trying to accomplish. It may have been easier, but I knew it would have also been fleeting. I wanted to make it on my own merits. Now I've been in this game more than fifteen years and am still on top.

I know there are quite a few women in other markets holding down their spot on their own merits. But none are doing what I'm doing in the media capital of the world—New York City. In a lot of ways, many female jocks coming up today are cheap imitations—Wendy wanna-bes. And I respect them, too, because once upon a time I was a Carol Ford wanna-be. That was the person I looked up to, whose career path I wanted to take. I remember when Carol Ford came to New York doing afternoons on KISS-FM. They brought her in with billboard ads and subways ads. She was a black woman with her own show and she was very well paid. They even put her up in a fancy hotel. She came into New York diva style. At the time I had just started college in Boston and I would spend whatever money I had whenever I had it on a train ticket to New York City. I would get to the city by two in the afternoon to tape Carol Ford's entire shift. I would sit in Grand Central Station with my Walkman recorder and headphones and listen and record. When it was over I would hop on a train back to school.

Those tapes were my training tools. I was committed to being good and being good meant learning from the best. Carol Ford was my role model. Before her, women on the radio were soft and sexy. They spoke in these muted tones and everything was soft and pink. But Carol Ford was loud and big. She had voices and characters. She used sound effects. She carved her own image, her own niche. She made radio fun and she seemed to be having fun doing it. I always knew that if I was ever going to go into radio I would have to carve my own niche and be different from every other woman out there. I always knew that I had to be a standout. And I am today. But I don't rest on my laurels. I don't take my position for granted. I can't relax and think this will always be here for me like this.

I know that part of a bitch getting a shot at dethroning me is getting a chance to sit in the big chair, filling in for me when I'm on vacation. Fuck that! Nobody's sitting in my big chair, not if I can help it. And *don't* get a bitch to sit in the big chair who is halfway decent and will also suck a dick. *What?!* And don't get a bitch to sit in the big chair who is halfway decent, willing to suck a dick and will take a fifty-thousand-dollar salary as opposed to my salary? Shi-it! I better never call in sick. I know those bitches are out there. I understand that a girl who will suck a dick and take a fifty-thousand-dollar paycheck and can do a cheap knock-off of me can snatch my spot. Those in positions to hire and fire like them cheap with big titties and aiming to please. Make no mistake. It's sad to say, but welcome to entertainment. That's why I don't give people the opportunity to sit in my seat. I make sure my ass is there every day.

It's a great feeling to know that I never lost (and God forbid if I ever lose) my ability to recognize the importance of showing up.

I never want to get to the point where I put my hands on my hips and say to myself, "You know what? I'm taking off because I deserve this! I don't feel well today and I'm not going in!" *What?!* How dare I?! I must come to work every day and be on my game.

Part of getting and keeping a job—any job—is showing the fuck up. People do not understand that. And until they do, people will continue to be unemployed. Some people have this twisted idea that nobody can do their particular job better than they can. They think, "Nobody can work this computer like me. They can't fire me." But the boss is thinking, "You know what? It's great you can work this computer very well, but if you are going to continue to show up late every day or call in sick every other month or have these excuses for not showing up, like your baby is sick or your ride keeps breaking down, I'd rather hire a lesser person who I'm sure will be here every day, on time."

Reliability is just as important as the other qualifications. And, no matter what has been going on in my life, I have always been reliable. Through inexperience and being wet behind the ears, through rape and abortion, even through cocaine addiction, I showed up. I could have had walking pneumonia and would still show up. To this day (and I have earned my stripes and can take the occasional day off whenever I want), my bosses still have to get on me to take my days. But now it's not just about being reliable for me. I'm addicted to my audience. I don't want to be away too long from my people, my listeners, my flock. They make me feel bad when I take off. They scream at me through faxes and phone calls. They don't like fill-ins. No disrespect to anyone who has ever sat in my seat, but people who tune into *The Wendy Williams Experience* expect Wendy Williams. They don't want some cheap imitation. They want me. They don't even want the "Best of . . ." *The Experience*. They want me. Live. And that's a great feeling.

I am not delusional. People who get delusional about their position—and I'm not talking about just radio and entertainment people, I'm talking people in any job, relationship or whatever—thinking they have it on lock are in for a rude awakening.

I have somehow always known that. I saw it—even before I knew what I wanted to do. It was part of my futuristic vision—my ability to see into my own future and act out scenarios of my life long before they actually happened. I attribute my success today to futuristic vision.

I've had it since I was very young. My futurist vision came from being an outcast in every single aspect of my life. I was a misfit basically from the time I came out of the womb. My parents are perfect. My sister, Wanda, who is seven years older than I am, is perfect. My brother, Tommy, the only boy and namesake to my father, is perfect. Then there is me—the big girl in a family of perfect bodies, the academically challenged child in a family full of academic achievers. I was an outcast in my own home, and when I got to school I didn't quite fit in anywhere there, either. I was the black girl in a practically all-white school. And among the handful of blacks, I was the "white girl," the outcast.

I spent most of my youth in my room, rocking back and forth for endless hours, plotting my future. I knew that one day my being different would pay off. I knew one day my size would pay off. I knew one day that the way I spoke, which made the black kids call me "white girl," would pay off. I knew one day what my parents felt was inappropriate talk would somehow pay off. All the things that set me apart and made me an outcast would work in my favor.

Even if no one else could see it, I could. I plotted on everything from the most simple—how I was going to tackle the Macy's One-Day Sale the next day and how I would navigate through the store—to the more complex, what type of woman I would be when I grew up and what kind of career I would have.

I learned early that you must see yourself in a position in order to be in that position. If you can't see it, you can't be it. It just won't happen for you. My brother coined the phrase "futuristic vision." He was my best—and only—friend growing up and I would share with him a few of my plans. I would tell him that one day I would be a radio personality or news anchor. I first wanted to be a newscaster, the woman who sits behind the desk and reads the news off of a TelePrompTer. But once I realized how restrictive that job was, that was it. I knew my personality was too big to sit behind some desk reading from a TelePrompTer. I knew I would be a personality even before I knew what that meant.

When my brother Tommy and I were very young I used to force him to play "Roving Reporter," a game I made up where I would interview him for my imaginary show. I think we played the game every day for an entire summer until he was sick of me.

Tommy wasn't only my interviewee, he was the one person who I would let in on some of my most intimate plots for my future.

"Wendy, you're always talking about things that aren't going to happen for like twenty-five thousand years," he would say. "You and your futuristic vision!"

Futuristic vision was my driving force. I never used it for destructive things. I never said in my quiet times, "Hmm, let me figure out a way to be disruptive," or "Oh, I'm going to drink and smoke or wild out in school to get attention." I always used my solitude to say, "I'll show them!" It was a positive "I'll show them." I wasn't trying to make anyone pay; I simply wanted people to see me the way I saw myself.

I wanted them to know that even if they didn't think I was cool and even if I didn't fit in that being me was okay. I also wanted to let all the other misfits out there know that being a misfit is exactly what you need to be to win in this world. You can't trip just because you're a little overweight or because you're not in the most popular clique because look at those skinny popular bitches today. Where are they now? If you have a face full of zits in high school, don't trip. They will go away and even if they don't they can't stop you if you truly have a plan for your life.

If you're a sixteen-year-old single mother, don't fret. While that wasn't my situation I know you can still achieve your goals and find strength through adversity. The battle rages on.

What I learned is that if you make mistakes, learn from them and move on and above all else be true to yourself—don't try to fit into a mold of what someone else thinks you should be.

I just kept being myself until the rest of the world caught up with me. When I was growing up I was teased and called "white girl" primarily because of the way I speak. The way I speak on the radio today is the way I spoke in Wayside when the black kids teased me. Today I am making loads of money because of the way I speak. I'm as "white" now as I was back then in terms of my delivery. Actually I'm as black now as I was back then. They just couldn't see me. I'm sure if you polled the black kids in my school they would say, "Yeah, Wendy will definitely marry a white guy." They didn't have a clue about me. While I was never a racist, white simply has never been my flavor.

But I guess I had to show them, just like I showed my parents that being a big girl would not hold me back. All the battles surrounding my weight were so unnecessary. Those talks, the diets, the looks, the comments didn't help me lose weight; it just made me feel bad about myself. But in my futuristic vision I knew. I knew that one day I would show them that a big girl could handle hers. Just give me a moment to get from under this tuna fish and mustard diet and I'll show you that size can be a plus, not a negative.

I envisioned how my career path would be. When I was in high school I used to talk about it so much that Liz, one of my closest friends, believed me. She would tell everyone, "You know Wendy is going to come back to the reunion in a purple Cadillac, with a long purple mink coat and she is going to be a deejay."

She was close. I didn't have a purple Cadillac or the mink (not yet). But I was a deejay.

I got my first New York City radio job at HOT-103, a dance-music station when I was about a year out of college. When my five-year high school reunion rolled around I was too pleased to go back to Ocean Township High School and show them. Many of my classmates had either dropped out of college or were still trying to finish or trying to find a job and I was already a big-time New York jock. (Yeah, I was working overnights, but I was on my way.) I showed up in all of my fabu-losity. I came back with flair— big hair, long pink nails and loud. I fulfilled my vision for myself.

I saw things when no one else could and I didn't just stop at the futuristic vision, I went out and did the damn thing. Now bitches are practicing every day to do my shit, the way I practiced to do Carol Ford's shit. They want a chance to sit in the big chair. But you can't get to this chair—not my chair—not without futuristic vision.

CHAPTER 1

Wendy from Wayside

WHAT MOTHER AND FATHER GIVE their daughter ruby earrings for getting her period? I got my period when I was thirteen. It was one of the most memorable and humiliating experiences I have ever had. I didn't get a box of pads and that little talk with my mother that most people get. No, both my mother *and* my father (how mortifying) sat me down for the "you're becoming a woman now" speech and afterward they presented me with two 14-karat gold birds with small rubies inside the claws of the birds. I guess the rubies were to signify my period and my passage into womanhood. My period seemed a bigger deal to my parents than it was to me.

I was not raised in a normal household. I'm sure my parents, Shirley and Thomas, will consider themselves the epitome of normal. But to the outside world, in many respects, I had the perfect family. And actually, looking back, I think so, too. I had a wonderful upbringing and I wouldn't trade my parents for any in the world. But . . .

Remember that song from *Electric Company*, "Which of these

11

things does not belong here, which of these things is not the same . . . ?" I was the thing that didn't belong in my family. That was what I thought growing up. Today, I know that's not true. I now know that I am definitely my parents' child and I totally fit with everything they tried to instill in us. It just took thirty-something years for me *and* them to realize it.

My parents worked very hard to give all of us a solid foundation. They worked extremely hard to make sure none of us wanted for anything. That was why we moved to Ocean Township, New Jersey—Wayside to be exact. We moved there when I was five from Asbury Park, which was going through a rough period following the riots. Moving to Wayside was like the Jeffersons moving to the East Side to a "deluxe apartment in the sky."

Wayside, a middle-class to upper-middle-class section of Ocean Township, was approximately forty-five minutes south of Manhattan on the Jersey Shore. There were people in our neighborhood with lots of money living in big houses. There were people living in big houses with money to live in bigger houses. And then there were people like my parents, who scraped together everything they had to give us the best. Part of the best included living in a nice, safe neighborhood without a lot of transient families. Wayside was usually the last stop for most families—people rarely moved from there. I had a next-door neighbor, Jackie, who was there when we moved in and was still there when we both graduated from high school and went off to college. She might be still there today for all I know. My parents wanted a sense of permanence for us and Wayside was that place.

My parents always traveled in the "right" circles. They were involved in many social activities and charities. And they had plenty of prominent friends, like Gwendolyn Goldsby Grant, a noted therapist who does an advice column for one of the major black magazines. She pledged AKA with my mother in college.

My parents weren't rich; they practically cut off their wrists for us to live the way we did. In fact, my parents always drove an old car when I was growing up—the kind you wanted to park down the street or around the corner out of embarrassment. They didn't waste money on showy material things. They saved and sacrificed for things that would advance our family.

We had a nanny/housekeeper, Mrs. Mary Johnson. We didn't have Mrs. Johnson because we were rich. We needed Mrs. Johnson because both of my parents worked and they didn't want us to be latchkey kids. My parents taught all week, graded papers, prepared for meetings and the like; it behooved them to have someone come in and clean and iron, too. So there was always Mrs. Johnson.

But we didn't have it like that. Not like the rich people down the street. They had a *live-in* nanny *and* a housekeeper. And those kids down the street were terrible to their help. They would do things like lock their nanny out in the freezing cold with no coat. If we even thought about disrespecting Mrs. Johnson we would get the hell slapped out of us. Besides, Mrs. Johnson did not play that.

My parents struggled so that my sister, brother and I wanted for nothing. We traveled. We shopped. Christmas was always big at our house. A typical Christmas for me would be four pairs of Calvin Klein jeans, a diamond floating heart, a teddy bear with a diamond belly button, lots of gold jewelry and makeup by Estée Lauder—never makeup out of a drugstore. My sister would get more of the same, just in smaller sizes. And my brother would get clothes that might include a whole collection of Izod shirts—one for every day of the week. My mother, though, was the queen of the discount shopping and while she would spend money, she would also wait until things went on sale.

I compare my family to the Cosbys, America's family when I was growing up. I was Denise, Lisa Bonet's character—the troubled middle child. My sister Wanda, who is seven years older than I, was Sondra, the Sabrina LeBeauf character on *The Cosby Show*. She was the smart, perfect daughter. Then there was Tommy, Theo Huxtable—the only boy in the family.

Wanda and I shared a room when Tommy was born and he was given my room. Wanda was the best big sister when I was young. She would often sneak downstairs late at night and bring back snacks for us. We would have orange slices or the little pizzas that you make in the toaster. We would play kicking-feet on the bed and she would ride me around on her back pretending to be an elephant. I was three and she was ten and entertaining her baby sister.

Then it just all stopped. As Wanda was moving into her teens and got into her grades and into her friends and into her life, those days of sneaking snacks, kicking-feet and playing elephant were fading. Who wants to hang around a little kid when you're becoming an adult? And from my perspective, who wants to hang around a perfect big sister and get lectured on your grades and behavior? Not me.

Tommy, who was only three years younger than me, became my best friend and confidant. He was my partner in crime and the only one who completely understood me—even to this day. I remember when we were kids I would make matching tee shirts using glitter and waterproof Magic Marker. My shirt read "machine wash" and his read "tumble dry." On another set of shirts I wrote "frick" on mine and "frack" on his. We would skip along the Belmar Beach arm and arm—tighter than Frick and Frack.

My sister had become the "Myth of Wanda"—I could no longer relate to her. We were sisters but with little in common. And by contrast she pushed me further into being a misfit. Wanda was the perfect daughter. She was quiet and understated. She dressed conservatively in muted tones and wore Birkenstocks. She had a perfect build—five-feet-six and a size six. She was a straight-A student, who left for Tufts at age sixteen on an academic scholarship.

I was nothing like Wanda. She was soft-spoken. I spoke too loud, too fast and too much—so much so that my parents had codes for me when I was in public or at social gatherings. We could be in a room full of people—if my parents said, "Wendy, TM!" that meant that I was talking too much or giving too much information. It was nothing for me to strike up a conversation with a perfect stranger and tell them about a fight I had with my mother that day because I gained weight. No subject was off limits. My loose lips were enough for my parents to have codes for me. TF was for too fast. I used to talk a mile a minute. I've learned to pace myself now. I have learned to use pregnant pauses for dramatic effect but I still have to think about it. And sometimes even today when I get caught up in a frenzy I revert back to that ten-year-old who talks too fast.

Then there was TL for too loud. I still talk too loud today. My husband is constantly signaling me to lower my voice because I have a tendency to speak really loud in public and draw attention to myself. When I was younger, my parents were constantly telling me, "Wendy, TL!" If we were out at dinner or something the codes would be followed by kicks under the table.

Wanda was the perfect size, I had a weight problem. I was a big girl—five-feet-eleven by the sixth grade, wearing a size eleven shoe. Actually my mother used to buy me a size ten because she had a hard time finding elevens back then and I would curl up my toes to fit into the tens.

Wanda's style was low-key, mine was loud and colorful. Remember the "Bedazzler," a kit that allowed you to adorn your clothes with rhinestones? I had a Bedazzler in the fifth grade and became the Bedazzler queen. I would take a plain denim jacket and fill it with intricate rhinestone designs. I would bedazzle everything from tee shirts to jeans. I graduated from bedazzling to painting on my clothes. I would rip up my tee shirts to create "one of a kinds." I had my own flair even at ten. If I was a guy I guess I would have been gay but not just gay, I would be a drag queen because I loved the flair. I know my conservative family was wondering where in the hell I came from—especially following Wanda.

The Myth of Wanda was something that I could never live up to. So I never tried. I never tried to be the anti-Wanda, either. I didn't go out on a limb to distinguish myself from her. In fact, I looked up to Wanda. She was the model. She set the mark for me and I appreciated that. I knew if I went too far away from that mark, I would be in trouble. So while I never tried to be like Wanda, I never moved too far away from the standards she set.

She went to the cotillion and was on the student council in high school. I never had the GPA to be involved with either. But I admired her for doing it. I never put any pressure on myself to try and follow in her footsteps. For one, my feet were too damn big. Secondly, I was that Lisa Bonet character. I marched to my own drum. When I realized early on that I was not going to be a straight-A student, I didn't stress myself about it. When I knew I wasn't going to be five-feet-six and a size six, I didn't stress myself. I always hated beige, I liked pink and hot pink at that. I wasn't conservative or understated, I was loud and big—I liked big hair, big nails, rhinestones and four-inch pumps. I was different.

I was a misfit outside of my home, too. I remember being bigger, taller and blacker than everyone in school. I also remember just when girls were thinking about boys, I was not a part of those conversations because the boys weren't thinking about me. I was the outcast.

Growing up I was invited to a few sleepovers but that's only because my mother was friends with the mother of the kid having the sleepover. Most of the time, I wasn't invited. When you have a sleepover your mom usually only lets you invite five people—five of your closest friends. I was never in anyone's top five. I might be in the top fifteen, at best, but I was never in the top five. And it hurt.

I was usually the only black in my class throughout school. When I graduated high school, I was one of four. One of the four ended up being in and out of the criminal justice system after graduation. He might even be dead now. And the other two didn't really speak to me much. I was the "white girl" to them. I didn't eat at the black table (as small as it was) because I didn't believe in succumbing to peer pressure.

I was liked by the white people in my school and, for the most part, I liked them. I just thought they had a twisted view of black people. They bought into the stereotypes and because of that they, too, excluded me from the black race.

They would from time to time refer to one of the black kids in our school as a "nigger" right in front of me and quickly say, "Oh, not you, Wendy." To them I wasn't a "nigger." I guess they thought the disclaimer, "Not you, Wendy," was some sort of a compliment like I would feel good about them saying nigger and then excluding me from being a nigger. I seemed to assimilate. I spoke a certain way. I dressed the way they did. They were so comfortable (too comfortable) that they used the word "nigger" and somehow knew it wouldn't insult me. But what they didn't realize was that telling me, "Not you, Wendy," was more of an insult than if they had called me a nigger because once again it set me apart.

Eventually, I found a group of misfits just like me when I got to high school. They were all white, though. There was a friend who was a relative of the former owner of the New York Jets. She was a punk rocker before it was cool to be a punk rocker. A lot of people considered her the freak of our class. She wasn't a bad kid. She wasn't into heavy drugs or anything. But she did have a fake ID, and drank and hung out at Hitsville, a punk rock club right across from the Stone Pony in Asbury Park. This friend had a convertible Mustang, which to me was very cool. There was also Diane and Liz. Diane was not so much a visual punk rocker as she was a mental punk rocker. And Liz was the quiet one. All of these girls were smart, straight-A students who still managed to punk rock and hang out. I was the girl who could talk and got Cs, and sometimes Ds. And a couple of times I would find myself in the little class at the end of the hallway with about six other kids—if you know what I mean.

Today when I go to schools to speak, I don't focus on the kids who are getting the As. And I'm definitely not talking to the ones with the perfect bodies because they get enough attention. I'm speaking to the kids who get the Cs and Ds and Fs—the ones who get railroaded into the "stupid" classes. And I'm talking to the girls with the bad body images and the lone blacks in white situations. Those are the ones who need the support.

I know because I didn't really get a lot of academic support at school. I had a guidance counselor who pretty much had me written off. As a matter of fact, I was a blow-off appointment for her, a waste of her time because she was busy trying to get the white students with straight As into college. She was annoyed to even have to spend a few minutes with me. They were the most discouraging few minutes I had ever spent. She told me my SAT scores were too low to get into college and my grades were even worse. She also told me that out of three hundred and sixty-three kids, I was going to graduate number three hundred and sixty and that I should think about trade school. Trade school? And she was serious.

But fortunately, I had my parents. Both of my parents were educators. My mother was a schoolteacher and my father was a school principal who later became an English professor at Monmouth College. He was like Roscoe Lee Brown on *A Different World*, very distinguished, good looking and a sharp dresser. My father is also very funny with a dry, sarcastic wit. He's the type to make you proud to say, "There's my dad!"

He and my mother always seemed to be pursuing some higher academic achievement. My mother got two masters degrees while we were growing up. And my father was working on his doctorate. Their academic excellence seemed to rub off on everyone, except for me. Wanda not only graduated from Tufts but also went to law school and became a successful lawyer. Tommy also went to school with grants and scholarships. In the Williams household, going to college, well, that wasn't even a thought. You were going to college.

My parents knew that for me, however, college wouldn't be so easy. They had to save for my college education because there was no way I was getting any kind of academic scholarship and my grades were too low to qualify for grants. My parents had a plan for me. I was the one they needed to make provisions for. I was their pet project.

They knew from day one that my sister would go on and do something brilliant with her life. And she did. They never worried about her future. As far as my brother, even if he didn't do well, he was still a boy and parents tend to feel that boys will always do okay in the world—after all, it is a man's world. Tommy also ended up being successful. He is a schoolteacher today.

"But what are we going to do with Wendy? What will become of her?" That was my parents' lament. I was never a good student. In the third grade I was getting notes on my report card saying, "She doesn't apply herself," which, in my case, was code for, "She's not very bright." By then my parents were already thinking, "Okay, we better start planning and stacking our chips. She clearly will not go to Harvard but we don't want her to go to community college, either."

My parents made sure that I would have a safety net. They made sure that my college would be paid for with no loans because they had no idea that I would even get a job making enough money to pay back those loans. They didn't want to set me up to fail. I don't even think my parents had high hopes of me marrying well—which was another option for a girl who wasn't an achiever in the classroom. While I've always been a cute girl, I had the weight factor. And we all know in life that cute in the face is not enough—you also have to be tight in the waist. If you're heavy, you may be fine to date but when well-appointed men are thinking about marriage they are looking for an arm piece. I wasn't arm-piece material (I am today, by the way). That's why my college education was paid for and I was also given a brand-new car, a Subaru, for graduation—just in case. My parents' minds were at ease because, at the very least, I would have a degree to get a job and a car to get to that job.

I am grateful to my parents for having enough foresight to know that without their planning I might not have ever gone to college. They were great examples and great teachers in how to survive in this world. The biggest lesson they taught me was the importance of presenting a good package. My parents knew how to present a good package to the world. That's something that too many young people today just do not get.

All of the saving and scrimping in the world would not have gotten me into college (not with my grades) if I did not present a good package. Colleges do not necessarily select students based on grades and scores but on their ability to mix in with the rest of the student body. My parents taught me that if I was well rounded, if I participated in activities in and out of school that I would have a better chance at getting into a college. Colleges are looking for well-rounded students who can add something to their school.

I had bad grades but I was a Candy Striper, helping out my local hospital. And I was a Girl Scout. I figured if I'm going to be failing just about every subject, I'll be a corny Girl Scout. I was getting kicked out of math class for failing so I had to do the extracurricular activities. No, I did not enjoy being a Girl Scout. Looking back they were a cross between lesbian and corny. They were boy-girls and I did not relate. I did not want to be eating smores around a fire with a bunch of bugs in a tent.

I was even on the swim team. Yes, my lazy behind was on the swim team, getting up early in the morning before school to practice. Why? Because I was going to get into somebody's college and being on the swim team—not the basketball team, not cheerleading or softball—looked better on my record. It wasn't a typical sport and it made me a standout. It gave the college admittance people something to add to that perfect package. I never won any swimming championships but I was good enough to be on the team and swim in the meets and I was good enough to get a partial scholarship to Boston College (which I did not take).

Another part of my perfect package was the way that I spoke. Even if you're not a whiz in the classroom there is no excuse for not being able to speak well because that's simply emulation and effort. Being able to speak well for me was a big plus. It's fine to know all the slang and have all of that street language down, but you must also know how to flip it and speak the Queen's English when you need to. No one ever told me this. No one had to. Growing up in Ocean Township and in my household, speaking with clear diction—pronouncing the entire word—was the norm.

My parents made sure that I had a personal interview with every school I applied. They knew I couldn't get in based on my transcripts. They knew that despite my poor grades, I could handle myself very well in an interview because I was used to speaking and I spoke well. Both of my parents would take off of work to accompany me on the interview to make sure that the package was intact. I would show up in my Izod shirts, maybe a plaid skirt or a pair of Gloria Vanderbilt jeans, a pair of Mary Janes or Polo loafers, my Farrah Faucett flip.

I sat in front of them as Wendy from Wayside with a parent on each side as a double minority. I got accepted to every school to which I applied. I got into schools that I was not qualified to get into and I'm not ashamed to admit that, because while I was not necessarily qualified to get into Northeastern, the school I eventually chose, I graduated from the five-year school in four years. Today I wave the flag of academic inadequacy high because people need to know that poor grades do not necessarily mean failure. Not if you know how to present the perfect package.

That perfect package got me over most of my life and was one of the reasons why I was able to succeed (even through cocaine addiction). I knew how to present the "package" no matter what the reality. I was a poor student from a hardworking family, but my package said affluence and intelligence. I was dabbling in drugs and alcohol in high school, but the package I presented was that of a good girl who would never do those things. I was able to fool everyone—including my parents.

I couldn't wait to go to college because I knew that finally I would be able to find people who were like me and perhaps find a crew, like the one my sister had at Tufts, which would totally accept me. I used to visit Wanda all of the time and those visits were the reason why I not only wanted to attend college but also attend college in Boston. I even had my first real kiss from a boy who attended Tufts. I met him at the school and told him I was seventeen. I was actually thirteen. He was very handsome and charming. We had our first kiss on an Amtrak train. He kissed me with his tongue and I could feel my breasts sprouting on the spot. I thought, "This is what it feels like to be a woman?! I like it!"

I don't think I ever spoke with my first kiss again and that didn't matter. He fulfilled his purpose in my life. He gave me a glimpse into my future. I couldn't wait to get to college where I could finally be free to be me. I couldn't wait to get to Boston where I had so many choices. I could date men from Harvard and men from MIT, men at Boston College and men at the University of Boston. There were so many colleges in the area and I chose Northeastern because it was so large that I could get lost in the numbers. It was not unusual for there to be classes with three hundred students. If I didn't show up, the professor would never know.

My mother, father and Tommy drove me to Boston (Wanda was in law school in Washington, DC) in the Lincoln Town Car. By this point, my parents had graduated from the embarrassing hoopdie into something more respectable. On the entire ride up I-95, I was so excited I thought I would burst. We pulled onto campus and up to my dorm and my mother managed to turn my excitement into fear. My mother is very, very social (which I hate) and she was talking and getting to know what seemed like every damn person on campus. It turned out that there were a lot of AKAs on campus helping the freshmen move in.

My mother is an AKA, my sister is an AKA, my sister-in-law is an AKA, my father is an Alpha, my brother is an Alpha, my brother-in-law is an Alpha. Of course, my mother just knew I was going to pledge. So as my mother was talking and being Miss Social, I could feel the AKAs looking at me like a piece of steak. I could almost hear them thinking, "Oh, yeah, we're going to get this bitch because we know she's going to want to pledge."

And there was my mother telling them, "Yes, Wendy is definitely going to want to pledge AKA."

Pledging was the last thing on my mind. I wasn't willing to go through any humiliating experiences. But I was torn because I also knew that I would never fit in with my family if I didn't. Pledging AKA would be the perfect way for me to finally find a group of girls who were just like my mother and my sister. So I considered it for two seconds.

But shortly after being in college—and I mean shortly, like less than six minutes—I realized that this pledging thing was not going to work out. Those bitches expected you to be at their beck and call. They would borrow your shit and not return it and I watched some of them even sleep with each other's men. And all that "Yes, Big Sister" shit. That was just not for me. I couldn't do it.

So I was back to my solitude. My college roommate was a lesbian who played sports and we had nothing in common so I spent most of my time in my room smoking weed, drinking and plotting my next move. I left for college with a carton of cigarettes and a shoebox full of weed. It was on like that. I started smoking cigarettes in high school with Leslie. She smoked Marlboros. But I smoked Newports. When my friends smoked cigarettes they bummed off of each other. I never wanted to bum anything from anybody. That was also the reason why I risked everything and drove my parents' car to Westlake Avenue in Asbury Park and Long Branch and took the train to New York to Washington Square Park to buy nickel bags of weed every week. I started buying them from my senior year until it was time to leave for college.

I first smoked weed, surprisingly enough, with some black girls—the same ones who were calling me white girl. Our town was so small there was really no room to run away from anyone. There was no room for them to call me white girl and then escape from me. We finally called a truce.

After smoking with them I decided that we had that one thing in common but it wasn't enough to forge a friendship. They knew girls that were having babies and for me that was another life. They spoke like adults and were all having sex. I might have still been a virgin. The only thing that we had in common was that we were black females from Ocean Township, and we smoked weed. That wasn't enough to be friends. But after that taste of smoking weed I decided I liked it enough to try and figure out how to get it on my own and avoid them. I started getting high finally with my white friends. But I got tired of smoking with them, too. I needed my own weed so I could smoke it by myself. I had plenty of money that I had saved when I got a windfall from the most unusual and tragic of circumstances several years prior. I was thirteen years old and I was visiting my grandfather who lived in Elizabeth, New Jersey. Papa lived on the first floor of a two-family house and his mother, my great-grandmother, lived on the second floor.

But as she started getting up there in age and getting sickly, she was moved downstairs with my grandfather so that someone would always be around to watch her. When I visited, I often took care of my great-grandmother. On one particular afternoon I was home alone with her and she had to go to the bathroom. I helped her get on the commode. She was so frail that she had to be helped onto the commode and watched until she was finished. She sat there for a minute and then leaned forward with her elbows on her knees, the way you might lean if you're taking a good, stiff shit. Her head bobs forward and I see her dentures rush to the front of her mouth. They are somehow dangling from her mouth, but they never fall completely out.

"Grandma?" I nudge her and she doesn't move. She was dead. Well, I'll tell you, beyond the tears there was something very comical about this situation and I don't think I'm going to hell for telling this story because she lived a full, happy life.

But I'm standing there freaking out not knowing what to do. I called 911. And I somehow got her off the commode, got her bloomers back up and I was going to put her in the bed to wait for the people to come. I was straightening up her room, trying to fix up her bed and I pulled back the sheets to find just under the edge of the mattress so much money I didn't know what to do.

I was thirteen and I figured no one would care, least of all Grandma—who like a lot of older people didn't trust banks—if I helped myself to some of the money. So I did. It was thousands of dollars—some Confederate bills, old coins, fifties, hundreds, singles. I grabbed about ten thousand and there was still plenty left over.

I tricked some of it up shopping at Bamberger's (which was Macy's before Macy's), and Debs and Annie Sez. I even called one of my best friends, Regina, one of my neighbors who was black from a wealthy family. I would drag her along with me to the mall. I was smart enough to buy things that wouldn't arouse any suspicion. I never showed up home with some slutty outfit that would make my parents question, "Where did you get that?" I was mostly buying clothes that blended in with all of the other clothes in my wardrobe.

But how foolish did I look showing up at Bamberger's with Confederate money? One clerk even said to me, "Are you sure you want to use this money?" I had no idea how valuable that old money was and how much it would be worth. It was probably worth one hundred times its face value and there I am spending it up. No wonder no one ever called security, I'm sure they were exchanging it for regular cash and pocketing it themselves.

I managed to save most of the money, though, and when I discovered weed, I had plenty of money to buy it. I would buy a nickel bag or two every week. I knew I was going to college so I let the nickel bags stack up.

Now understand that I was in no way a Buddha head. I smoked weed for the first time in the eighth grade and didn't really smoke again until well into high school. I had never bought the stuff. I liked it but I was not into it like that. In fact, it only took a couple of pulls for me to get high. But I decided I liked it enough to make sure I had some when I went away to college.

I knew weed would be a part of the curriculum for me. And having my own supply wasn't about being a weed head as much as it was about being in control of my own shit. You may like Pop-Tarts or cookies and while you don't eat them all the time, you make sure they're in the cabinet, just in case. That's the way I felt about weed. When I wanted it, I wanted it to be available without exposing my wants to anybody else. So I planned ahead. I made sure I had enough to last me the entire school year; I needed it to. That was my futuristic vision at work. I had envisioned that I would be rolling with a certain kind of crowd. I saw my crew as black and I saw me as being a standout because my goal was to be a little wilder than the average chick. I had planned to go to college and attack the social scene—me and my shoebox full of weed.

I wasn't planning on being the campus slut or anything like that. I wasn't "that type" of girl, sexually. Hell, I didn't lose my virginity until I was seventeen going on eighteen and even that was carefully planned out. I knew I didn't want to go to college a virgin. I wanted to have fun in college and I didn't want to stress the virginity thing. Not that I wanted to be fucking everybody on campus, I just didn't want to be "the virgin." In college you know how you can kind of tell who is into what. And the virgin always sticks out.

I also knew I never wanted to get caught out there with a guy the way too many girls do when they go away for the first time.

You see it all the time. These girls who come from these sheltered backgrounds go away to college and fall in love with some guy. The next thing you know, the dumb bitch is ironing his shirts and cooking for his ass. She's playing homemaker in a dorm room or off-campus apartment and not taking care of her own business while he's doing whatever the fuck he wants. He's the captain of the basketball team and cheating like mad. And she is just ironing and cooking away. That was not going to be me.

I was not going to be macked. My futuristic vision told me I was going to be doing the macking. And I ended up being a mack-tress. While that chick was back in the room ironing jeans and shirts and shit, her man was in my room—smoking weed and drinking 40s. In my dorm, people had to sign in whenever they came to visit. Most of the time we were just smoking weed and hanging out. But I'm certain the people in charge of the sign-in book probably thought I was some sort of whore.

I was finding my place in college. But while I was fitting in socially I wasn't fitting in at all academically. I was up to my old tricks. At this point my life could have taken a turn for the wild, and my parents were totally in the dark about it because the same picture that I presented to the world they bought into. My parents bought the lie. If I wasn't smart enough to barely get into college, why would they believe that all of a sudden I became this genius? Why weren't they asking to see my grades? Why did they believe me when I would tell them that there was a holdup with the grades?

Grades eventually came home. But they weren't the grades I

actually had. I changed them and sent home my version of my academic achievement. Shouldn't all of those As and Bs and that 3.0 GPA have raised a red flag? In reality, I was barely passing. I could have flunked out at any given time in college. I did just enough work not to have to tell my parents that they were sending me home.

And it wasn't that I wasn't applying myself. I certainly was—to all the corrupt things. Well, not all the corrupt things. In the solitude of my dorm room one night, I discovered something that would change the course of my life. It was destiny. It was radio.

CHAPTER 2

Radio

I WAS SITTING ON THE FIRE escape outside of my dorm room taking a bottle of Old English to the head. It was freshman week at Northeastern and while every other freshman was at the "welcome to the school" parties and all that shit, I was in my usual place— alone.

I thought coming to college I would finally find my place. I would have this whole crew that liked to do the same things I liked to do. I knew early it wouldn't be the sorority types. I couldn't get with the Gucci-shoe types. I wasn't with the goodie-goodie types. I didn't even hang out with my roommate. She was nice and everything but we didn't have much in common. She had her crew— the athletic girls. Where in the hell were the "like to drink, like to smoke, like to laugh" crew? Where were they?

It seemed that all of the freshmen were all clean-cut, prim and proper. I grew up in a white town. I knew how to drink. I wasn't looking for "welcome to school." Where were the real parties? So there I was on the fire escape with my best friend—me—

getting fuuucked up on some weed and Old E, straight out of the bottle. I had a wet towel at the door so that none of the weed would escape into the hallway.

I decided to check out the radio stations around Boston to see where I wanted my preset stations to be and I came across the campus radio station, WRBB. There was a disc jockey on, named Irving, with that quiet storm chatter. For kicks, I decided I would call him. Back in Wayside I never got the chance to call a radio show, even though I always wanted to. They didn't have 800 numbers to stations back then and any calls I made to a station would show up on a phone bill. But I was in college now and I was paying the phone bill. (Yes, with my parents' money. But so what?) I was free, dammit! I was drinking, smoking and calling a radio station.

Irving picked up the phone and gave me the typical "Hey, baby!" talk that most men give to women late at night. They don't take us seriously even when we want to be taken seriously and I realized that even though I was the one high on weed and OE, I still wasn't one of those "Hey, baby!" types. I wasn't trying to date Irving; I was just looking for a little conversation and some fun. He invited me to the station, which was across campus.

"What the fuck," I thought. I wasn't doing anything special anyway.

I walked across campus to the station. I was intimidated by the whole scene at first. There were all these buttons and the mike and he was on the air. He was a senior—like a tenth-year senior— one of those seniors who are only a few credits shy of graduating but somehow never manage to graduate. He told me everything he knew about radio. I spent a couple of hours on his shift with him and loved every minute of it. I liked the power of the mike and being able to talk to people but not actually have them in your face. I liked the music and the atmosphere. I was hooked. I had found my niche. I found my place at Northeastern.

Irving and I became friends and I quickly got into the radio clique. I found a new bunch of misfits. Irving wanted to be a Kappa but he didn't make it and ended up on the radio. Crystal, who lived downstairs from me in the dorm, was one of those "happy to be here" kind of chicks. I called her a "Suzy-type." There was another jock that wanted to be an Omega Psi Phi man and didn't make it; another wanted to play on the basketball team and got cut. And there was me. I was proud to say that I was one of those misfits. And not much has changed. Today I am part of the radio industry, but I still don't quite fit. I will go to the parties, look around and say to myself, "I'm so not a part of this." Then I go to parent-teacher conferences and I look around and I say, "I'm so not one of you, either."

I started at my college station reading the news. I thought I wanted to be a newscaster. But I discovered that there was much more out there for me. I started my very own shift. I called myself "Golden Girl." It was my sophomore year and I had returned to school following a vacation on Martha's Vineyard. I had put Sun-In in my hair, which made it look all cheap and bleached out but against my tanned skin, I looked golden. So that was my on-air name.

I loved being on the radio. I knew this was the career path I was going to pursue. I was a communications major at North-eastern, which is a five-year school. Under their system you are supposed to take two semesters to work or intern in your chosen field and then come back and graduate. But in my department I saw that they were offering internships at places that had absolutely nothing to do with radio, like Wang Computers or at record stores. I didn't want to fix computers or sell records. I wanted to be a fucking deejay. "Could you get me an internship at a fucking radio station?!" I would ask. "No?! Well then I'll do it myself."

Without asking my fellow deejays at the college radio station, I went out and got my own internship. I called radio stations in the area and asked for the personnel department. I told them I was looking to intern there and asked them what I needed to do. I knew when speaking to me they thought I was white. When I showed up and they saw I was black, I was practically hired on the spot. A black girl—a minority—who sounds white? I was in. I just capitalized on exactly who I am, knowing exactly where it will get me, and that's how I got my internship.

I interned on the morning show at KISS-108, the number one station in Boston. The morning host, Matty Siegel, who is still there today, was the number one jock in the city. I interned there while going to classes. Actually, I cut classes a lot of times to be there. This was going to be my big break—a break I created for myself.

An internship back then (and still today) consisted of getting coffee, making sure the jocks had whatever newspapers or faxes they needed and being a gofer. And I did that happily just to be around professional disc jockeys, just to be in that environment.

But I wasn't content just doing that. I knew if somehow I stood out, opportunities would present themselves to you. I would spend the night before doing my nails. I would either paint each finger a different color or have bright, bright red nail polish. When I had to do my little work at the station, like delivering contest sheets or other papers, I would make a big to-do with my hands so that they would notice my nails. I would make sure that I made my special deliveries during the show, when the mike was open. I did this because if they had any kind of manners I was certain to get a "Thank you, Wendy" on the air. And I got to say, "You're welcome, Matty!" on the air.

When I started doing outrageous things to my nails, the comments progressed from "Thank you, Wendy" to "Would you look at this! What have you done to your nails, Wendy?" And I would tell them. That led to them including me even more by asking, "What did you do last night, Wendy?" I guess expecting some outrageous answer. I did not disappoint. "Oh, I was watching *Dynasty* while doing my nails and did you see that fight between Alexis and Krystal . . ." as I proceeded to go into my patented enthralling, exciting, blow-by-blow recapping of the fight. That turned into a weekly on-air recap on what happened on *Dynasty*. I turned a little internship, being a gofer, into being a featured player on the number one–rated morning show in Boston. I started turning my recorder on before going into the studio for my little part.

At the same time, my shift on WRBB was jumping off big. I

had landed the most coveted spot on the station—the evening drive, from six to ten. They called that slot *Soul's Place,* and it was the most-listened-to time because most of the student body would be in their dorms chilling, listening to the radio. I was playing popular music like Earth, Wind & Fire, Cameo, the Gap Band and LL Cool J and I was all fun and giggles.

During my senior year, I was about to start applying for radio jobs across the country, when I received a call from a program director from Rochester. He had been passing through Boston and caught my show one evening and was very impressed. He left a message with my program director at WRBB to call him. I did.

"I want to offer you a job," he said.

I was absolutely gagging. The job that he wanted to offer me was a midday shift from ten in the morning until two in the afternoon. I couldn't even catch my breath before he offered to fly me to Rochester to discuss his offer. *Oh my God!* He sent me a plane ticket and the next week I was in Rochester. I didn't tell anyone around campus because I didn't believe it. I didn't tell my parents because this would mean that I wouldn't be graduating from college. It was Christmastime and if I accepted the job I would have to drop out of Northeastern, just months before graduation. And while I knew it was out of the question for a Williams to drop out of college, I figured, Why are you in college, anyway? To get a job, right? And here I was with a job offer.

I watched one of my fellow schoolmates and a WRBB jock, Diana King, drop out of Northeastern just two years prior to pursue her radio dreams. She landed a job at WBLS in New York. She was a couple of years older than me and she got a New York City deejay job. She set the precedent for me.

But on the plane ride to Rochester I hatched a plan. I could enroll at the University of Rochester as a nonmatriculating student and I could still get my degree from Northeastern. My parents would be happy and all of those years of struggling through Northeastern would not be in vain.

I arrived at the airport in Rochester. It was a snowy day and the program director, who happened to be the son of the station's owners, was there to meet me. I spent the week from the time he called me until the time I actually ended up in Rochester fantasizing about this meeting. I envisioned that they would pick me up in a limo and put me up in a fancy hotel like the Ritz Carlton in Rochester. I imagined the station would be in a high-rise building with all new state-of-the-art equipment.

I should have known that was just a fantasy when they flew me coach. The program director showed up in a Camry and drove me to the radio station. It was inside a big house, not much bigger than my campus station and a world away from KISS-108. That station was very upscale, with booming crystal-clear 50,000 watts. KISS-108 had money. The program director, Sonny Joe White, drove a Bentley. Matty Siegel drove a Porsche and wore all designer clothes. That was my idea of the big time. But who was I kidding, I was still in college, working at a college station and interning at KISS-108.

I was grateful for the offer. I was being plucked from my senior year. This program director told me that my starting salary would be thirty thousand dollars, which was great money just out of college. Everything happened so fast. He gave me paperwork, introduced me to the owners (his parents) and everyone else at the station. He hooked me up with a realtor and dropped me off at a local hotel, which was more like Motel 6 than the Ritz. But I was floating on cloud nine.

When I got to my room I called my parents to share my good fortune. This was the first time I had ever shared with them my desire to be in radio. I was Wacky Wendy. They knew about my show and internship but they figured I would graduate and go on and do something else. They looked at radio as a recreation, not a career. I gave them the full story. I told them I was staying in college, that I would attend the University of Rochester. Everything was positive. There was no pearl-clutching drama. They went along with it. The next day I went out and I started to look at apartments. I found a nice studio apartment in a building of garden apartments. I got back to my room and called my parents to tell them when I was going back to Boston to settle my affairs there. The Rochester station was going to pay for my first and last month security on the apartment, so I was practically set. Before I left I took a cab over to the University of Rochester campus and I found out about the enrollment. It would be no problem. I would be able to get my diploma mailed to me. I didn't care about the formal graduation ceremony, anyway. During my weekend in Rochester I even established a weed connection. There was a place called Chili—an urban area of the city near the projects. I drove over there and got a nickel bag to last me through the trip. This was going to be perfect.

Before I headed back to Boston my new boss picked me up, took me to breakfast and dropped me off at the airport. I would be starting the following month. On my plane ride back to Boston I was about to bust. My mind was racing. I was mapping out my future. I would have to dump my boyfriend. No need carrying old bags into a new situation. Was I going to be Golden Girl or Wendy Williams on the air? I was feeling really good about everything that was about to happen.

I decided I wouldn't tell my boyfriend it was over, I would just move to Rochester and the calls would get less and less frequent. He would figure it out. No need for a big confrontation. But back on campus, he was one of the first I told about my good fortune. I figured I'd ease my way out of it. Things would be going smoothly for me.

Two days after returning from Rochester I got a call from the program director there. He told me that the station was rescinding its offer. He said I took advantage of my hotel stay and made long distance calls. Well, I was absolutely floored. I felt as though I took advantage of no one. I made two calls. One to my parents, to tell them about my job offer, and another to my parents to let them know I was on my way back to Boston. There was no way we talked for hours. I'm not even a phone person, to this day. And if the bill was an issue, I would have been glad to pay. But they never gave me an opportunity. I thought dropping the offer for something like that was pretty petty. I wish the guy would have told me the truth. I think they had found someone local who would be cheaper to deal with. In-house talent is always cheaper. They wouldn't have to pay for moving expenses and all of that.

I cried for days. I never explained to my parents what happened. I told them that I decided not to take the job. Inside I figured if they were offering me this job while I was still in college, I would certainly get other offers.

I learned a valuable lesson from this experience: Nothing is guaranteed. People can change their mind at the drop of a dime and a lot of times you will have no recourse. I didn't curse anybody out. I couldn't sue. There was nothing I could do. All I could say was okay. And cry.

It was the late 1980s, I was a senior and I didn't let the loss of the Rochester job stop me. I knew I had a few months left to get busy and send out air checks and find a radio job. He could take away the job but he couldn't take away the complimentary things he said about my performance. He wanted me site unseen.

My air checks were a combination of WRBB-FM and my soap opera reports on KISS-108. One of my fellow jocks, Mike Shannon, helped me put them together because I didn't have a clue. I was able to repay the favor years later when I gave his air checks to my boss at KISS-FM in New York, where he's still a jock today.

I used *Radio & Records* magazine, a trade publication for the industry which has radio job openings, and sent out the tapes that Mike helped me put together all over the country. I got three offers back: Rehoboth Beach, Delaware; a station in a small town

in Illinois, about two hundred miles outside of Chicago; and I got
a job offer in St. Croix.

I was not scared whatsoever to pack up my bags and go where
I had to go to work.

I had no idea where the last stop in my radio journey would be.
But I thought I wanted it to be in Chicago or Atlanta. These were
two cities that I associated with having a strong, positive black
image. I wanted to be where the black people were doing the
damn thing. I wanted to be in cities where black success was cele-
brated, where there were black architects, doctors and congress-
men.

New York never even crossed my mind. I mean it was New
York—so big, so intimidating. It was out of my league. Go on, lit-
tle girl? Please. That was the town of Ken (Spider) Webb, Sergio
Dean, Carol Ford, Chuck Leonard and the legendary Frankie
Crocker. These people were not going anywhere unless they died.
Diana King managed to crack New York. But she was a New
Yorker. She got her job by persistently waiting downstairs at
WBLS for Frankie Crocker to come by. When he did, she
charmed him and gave him a tape. She was very smooth and per-
suasive. She got a part-time job, filling in—oftentimes for
Frankie's shift.

But no one was cracking New York. And Diana's was "I'm not
the one to pull muthafuckas in!" And I don't blame her. I would
be the same way. There's not room for everybody, dammit. Don't
ask me for favors until I get my feet firmly planted. She was tread-
ing water. I would go home and hear her filling in for Frankie

Crocker, the prime shift. I was very proud of her. But I would never call her to ask her for favors. I understood. People are looking to get their own shit going before even thinking about doing favors for others.

I chose the job offer on St. Croix because at least on St. Croix there would be some sunshine and I would meet all kinds of interesting people. The idea of being on an island was more appealing than being in a cornfield in Illinois, with no tourism, or in Rehoboth Beach, Delaware, some really white, really remote place.

The two mainland jobs were offering salaries like twelve thousand dollars a year for the midday shift.

WVIS, St. Croix—a soca, reggae and Calypso station—in the U.S. Virgin Islands in Frederiksted, St. Croix, was paying $3.25 an hour for my four-hour afternoon shift. I played hip-hop and R&B during my shift. This station wasn't much for format. Things were disorganized and I really never found a good working rhythm while there. In fact, I hated it. But I was determined not to let the experience on the island break me. I was away from my family and everything I loved on this strange island with even stranger people.

I spent eight months in the beautiful Virgin Islands basically as a hermit. I was very paranoid down there. I never went out and didn't do anything while there. I was celibate the whole time because I didn't want to establish myself with a gynecologist in the Virgin Islands. When you're sexing, you need a good gynecologist. You may have issues. You may get an infection. You may get pregnant—anything can happen. And I just didn't want to deal with any of the things that could physically happen by having sex, so I abstained from sex altogether.

While the island itself was one of the most beautiful places I had ever been, there was an underlying ugliness. Yes, there was the appearance of morality, family values and respect. But what I was seeing was women being played out, left and right on the island. I'm not making a judgment; I'm just telling you what I saw. Eight minutes into my stay there I saw what was going on and I said to myself, "I'm not fucking with any of you all." And I didn't.

I saw plenty that convinced me that I shouldn't be having sex. I saw married men hooking up with younger, more attractive women while their wives were home taking care of the kids, hanging clothes on the line and cooking for their man. I was twenty-one and hit on by men twice my age. I know I was perfect mistress material—young, unattached, no children and pretty.

I lived in the maid's quarters of the big house of these two doctors who were from Puerto Rico. I knew I didn't want an apartment of my own. And living inside a home gave me a little sense of family and safety. I felt protected in this gated community in the maid's quarters.

But outside those gates was trouble. Storms—which seemed to happen every day—would knock out the power and phone lines for hours. And if my car broke down I was worried that something dangerous would happen to the physical me rather than having the feeling that a local person might actually stop and help. I can say that because I lived there. That was my experience.

I made very little money and the cost of living made it even worse. A pint of Häagan-Dazs was $5.25. Everything had to be flown in. The only thing that was cheap was the rum. Magazines would be marked up about $2. *Elle* magazine had just come out during my senior year of college. I absolutely loved it. I would have to wait two weeks longer than any newsstand in the United States and when it did come, it was $4.25 down there—two dollars more than in the States.

Thank God for my parents.

When I told them that I was taking a job in the Virgin Islands, they were skeptical. But they wished me well. I knew inside they felt that this radio thing wasn't serious and that they were just humoring me until I came to my senses and settled into a "real" job.

My parents paid for my rent from the States. They bought me a beat-up Pinto because the Subaru they bought me for graduation cost about five thousand dollars just to ship it to the Virgin Islands. So it sat in my parents' driveway. And I guess my parents felt I would be home soon enough. From their perspective, I was the little lost girl, trying to figure out what I was going to do with my life. So they figured they would keep things ready for my quick return. I would still have my room and my car and "We will be here to hug her and encourage her." And all would be right with the world.

So there was no way I was going to tell them how I was really feeling about being in the Virgin Islands. I knew that I could not complain to them. Partly because I didn't want to hear any "I told you so," but also because I didn't want them worrying about me at all. I kept the things that made me fearful to myself. I didn't want to be forced to leave the island, or constantly worried about or ha-ha'd at by my friends. So my reports back home were always, "Oh, I'm having a great time." But there wasn't a day that went by that I didn't cry.

Oftentimes I cried right through my show, behind the scenes. But I knew how to pull it together and put on a good face. There was a beach there called Hay Penny Beach. And I forgot the guy's name but he was a chi-chi man—he was gay. I forgot how I met him but I know I gravitated toward him. He was nice to talk to. He didn't know much about mainland culture and he seemed to be always on the beach, raw. He never harassed me for sex or extra conversation. We would smoke weed together—he always had weed. I smoked weed with him every day. I would even smoke on the radio. And if he didn't show up, I picked fanta leaves from my backyard and smoked that. It would get me somewhat high.

From the very moment I said good-bye to my parents, I knew I would not come home until I had a real job in radio in the United States waiting for me. I knew it would happen. And I knew that my next job in radio would pay more than $3.25 an hour.

Months into my job at WVIS, I learned from *Radio & Records* magazine that there was a new radio station launching in New York and they were looking for jocks. They had been on the air but they had no jocks in place. Generally when new radio stations start, they start with nothing but music just to get in. The station was HOT-103.

I called directory assistance from my house and got the number to the station. I called and the secretary said they were taking tapes and gave me the address to send mine. Prior to leaving for the Virgin Islands, I had purchased a boom box with a dual cassette recorder and a pause button. I was very conscientious in doing near perfect mike breaks on the air because I did not know how to edit. The best I could do was record from tape to tape so my breaks had to be tight. I sent HOT-103 air checks just about every week. I would send one on Wednesday and then send one on the following Monday, then again on the following Tuesday. I bombarded this radio station with air checks. And once again, being a standout paid off. I didn't send my package in a regular envelope. I used my station's stationery—which was real colorful with a big palm tree on the front.

Every time I sent a package to HOT-103, I followed up with a call to the program director. I called every week. Finally one time I called and the secretary put me through to him. I told him who I was and what I was doing. He told me he liked listening to my tape and he only opened my package because of the stationery. It stood out and was interesting. In a sea of manila and plain envelopes my palm tree stood out.

"When you come back to the States," he said, "give me a call."

He gave me no promises but plenty of hope. I took that one little statement and ran with it. I zeroed in on working at HOT-103.

Along with sending my tapes to HOT-103, I was also sending them to other stations advertised in back of *Radio & Records*. I got a response from WOL-AM in Washington, DC. They played oldies and had a very low wattage. But I didn't care. I was hired by Neville Waters, the program director. WOL-AM was owned by Kathy Hughes, who wielded a lot of power in DC. She was (and still is) a bad B. She was big in DC politics and the social scene. She was very attractive, sassy and knew how to get what she wanted. WOL was her first station. Today she presides over the Radio One empire.

Neville said he hired me because he liked my tape and because I was cute. Yes, I sent a picture. They offered me a salary of nine thousand dollars a year and I took it without any argument or negotiation. I flew straight from St. Croix to DC. My parents met me in DC with the Subaru and I got an apartment.

DC was one of the top ten markets and I was focused on making a name for myself there. I was in the same market with Donnie Simpson, a radio legend, and Candy Shannon, the big woman in town. And I was this green kid who didn't quite seem to fit in with DC. That town was a hard nut to crack. To put it bluntly, DC was country. They had their favorites and they didn't take well to outsiders, which I was. It's like that in every market, though, especially New York. Now that I'm on the inside of New York, I totally understand the squeeze out.

"Hell, no, you can't just roll up in New York from California or Dallas and think you're taking over. You ain't just coming up in here running shit!" That's the attitude. "We have to at least have heard of you. Even if you're a washed-up R&B singer or a rapper, trying to do radio here, you better be from New York." We would rather have that than a strange jock from Los Angeles.

And that was cool, because I wasn't planning on staying in DC long, anyway. As soon as I touched down in DC, I let the program director at HOT-103 know that I was now working in DC.

"Boy, AM oldies?" he said.

"Yeah, I'm a true radio lover," I told him. "I was always under the impression that a true radio disc jockey could perform well under any format."

He needed to know that I was a true jock and that just because I was black didn't mean that I could only work at an urban station. I needed to show that I was flexible. And I think this program director liked that. I guess my wet-behind-the-ears, new-to-the-business naïveté intrigued him. He knew I wasn't going to come in like some diva bitch demanding all of this money and other perks.

While in DC I would send HOT-103 tapes about once a month. I was ready to leave because things were starting to get a little heated for me. I had started getting into the dating scene and was beginning to dabble in cocaine.

CHAPTER 3

The Jump-Off

I EXPERIENCED MY FIRST CELEBRITY encounter up close in DC. I dated a professional athlete named Brian Fisher (not his real name). Brian was the star of the Washington Redskins. I never followed football, so while I knew he was famous I had no idea what he did on the field. I had never seen him play. But everybody else seemed to know him well so it looked good for me to be seen with him. I was in my early twenties and on the rise and he was a star.

He picked me up at my apartment. He took me to dinner at Tacoma Station. He had a chocolaty complexion, a great body and was very handsome. We didn't get into any deep conversation over dinner; I just loved being out with him. I loved being seen with him. After the date he dropped me off home. I was looking forward to the next date.

The next day it was all over the station that I went out with Brian. Neville pulled me aside and said, "You do know he's married with a lot of kids, don't you?" I didn't. I had no idea that not only did he have children with his wife, but also with several other women. So despite attention and star treatment that was our first and last date. I couldn't see myself being anyone's mistress. I thought I deserved better than that. And thank God we never had sex.

My disappointment didn't last long, because the next week I found myself being wooed by another attractive, prominent man—a budding R&B singer. Even though we were an oldies station, we managed to play about three current songs an hour on my show and one of them was from this artist, who had a hit record at the time. He had a smooth, smoky voice and was quite attractive—about six-feet-four, light skinned and curly hair (which was in back in the '80s). He came to DC on a promotional tour for his album. And at the time I wasn't into gossip or else I would have gotten the lowdown on this singer.

Unbeknownst to me he had just been released from jail. I don't know what he went to jail for but it was common knowledge to everyone in the biz (except for me) that he had been locked up. Industry people weren't really talking to me like that then. I was an AM oldies jock who didn't really count. I was playing contemporary music on occasion but it didn't count as far as being "in the know." I wasn't Donnie Simpson, who back then wasn't talking to me, either. I'm sure he didn't know I existed. And I was too scared to talk to him. There were other big jocks in town with big reps. Famous and popular acts came to our station more as a favor to Kathy Hughes than for any kind of career boost for me and my show. We were by no means on the radar as a player in the business.

So it was exciting to have someone really popular come through. This R&B singer stopped by and I interviewed him for my show. He had a top-ten single, a beautiful song. (PS: We haven't heard from him since. He was a one-hit wonder.) He was handsome and he was flirting hard with me.

During this time I was on a cocaine diet that had me really slim. You know I had been struggling with weight since I can remember, since my mother put me on a diet in the first grade. But cocaine made my weight a nonissue. And I very much liked that.

I had dropped almost fifty pounds in no time at all. It was dramatic. Thank God I didn't have friends coming back and forth to DC who could say, "I was just here last week and you look like you dropped about ten pounds. What's happening with you?" I started out in DC about a size sixteen but within about two months I was down to a size six. My shift was from three in the afternoon until seven. I would do cocaine after the shift, practically all night and sleep until two in the afternoon. When I woke up I had to get ready to start my shift again. The only time I would eat was when I wasn't doing cocaine—which was becoming less and less frequent. And I was getting skinnier and skinnier.

I didn't think that I looked good, but I was the size I always thought I wanted to be. I was finally supermodel skinny, which meant to me that it was just a matter of time before I landed that job in New York or that man who had some money. Nothing could stop me. I was just cute enough to get into all the right circles—whether it was a politician or behind-the-scenes guy in entertainment or an entertainer himself. I was that hot. Hell, Jody Watley came to the oldies station and was looking at me like, "Bitch!" and I'm thinking, "You're Jody Watley giving me the look?! Wow!" She was actually threatened by me. I looked at that as a complete compliment.

I didn't flaunt it like I was the "it" girl. But in my mind I was thinking, "There's something to be said of this."

So while I'm interviewing this R&B singer, I am not surprised that he was flirting with me the way he was. I was doing the basic radio interview, throwing him soft questions like, "So what's your new album about?" And instead of answering my question he said, "Nobody told me that in this little AM station sitting on the corner of Fourth and H in DC I was going to find such a diamond in the rough."

"Ohhhhh, thank you!" I squealed. "Okay, now back to you."

"No, back to *you*," he said. "So how old are you?"

"Well I just graduated from college," I told him, thinking this was a big deal back then. In my industry it was a big deal. Now it's not a part of my résumé, it's just a sidebar. But back then I was only *too* proud to say, "Yes, I graduated from college and I'm single."

"You're single?"

"Yes," I said.

It went back and forth. And I liked it. I liked him, too. But I wasn't strong enough at that point to say to him, "Let's go out." Nor was I strong enough or bold enough in my cocaine habit to show him my package and divulge what I was really up to.

He finally asked me to go out with him when we went off the air. And I said, "Sure!"

He had a limo waiting for me when I ended my shift. We went out to dinner. After dinner we were supposed to go to one of these glamorous industry parties in DC. He told me that he needed to stop off at his hotel to change his clothes and he invited me up. I'm not thinking anything but that he was going to change his clothes and he wanted me to wait for him upstairs. I was thinking, "I'm about go to through the lobby of this swanky hotel with this hunky singer and look at me!" And while I was not a radio star, his name could land us in the society pages the next day. I figured that I was moving up one way or the other.

I was so naïve at this point. So naïve. I was thinking guys date girls like me for the purpose of marriage. I'm a nice girl from a two-parent household in New Jersey. I'm a college graduate with no children. I figured they saved all that dog stuff, all that hootchie stuff for the hootchies. That is why I also always kept my habit to myself because nice girls don't do cocaine. I knew aesthetically I was still a nice girl. I just had this secret habit.

I was a nice girl, with a college background, a college gradua-tion car, a mommy and a daddy and a room waiting for me in our modest home in rural, suburban New Jersey. I spoke nicely and I carried myself well—like a real high-society woman. Shit, I even went to charm school. I knew which fork to use and had impecca-ble table manners. I'm the girl you can bring home to your mother.

I'm thinking, "Now I'm walking through the lobby because he wants to show what a nice girl he's dating." And it doesn't hurt my career to be seen with him, either.

We get up to the room. And he starts changing his clothes. He starts taking off his pants right there. And at first I'm very uptight and nervous. But I said to myself, "Wendy, welcome to entertainment. You need to loosen the fuck up!"

But inside I'm screaming, "Oh my God! Celebrity penis!"

After he took his pants off he approached me as I was sitting on his bed and he forced himself on me. He didn't wear a condom and I didn't scratch and fight. But it was clear that I was not an active participant. I was date raped. After he was finished I left.

We never made it to that party. This man said nothing to me. And I said nothing to him. I just got up and left. There were no tears. I didn't call anyone. I didn't run downstairs crying through the lobby disheveled. I simply left.

I was so out of it I don't even know how I got home. I think I had a few dollars in my pocketbook and I must have taken a cab home. I got home and I soaked a washcloth in alcohol and bathed my privates. I douched with vinegar, hoping to douche everything away.

I know I was raped. But I don't compare it to the kinds of rape women experience around this world. I wasn't brutalized in an alley, my clothes weren't torn. What happened to me was classic date rape. I knew my attacker. Fortunately, I didn't know him well, where he could hurt me deeply emotionally, too. He wasn't a friend of three years who all of sudden turned on me like a wild dog. He was somebody involved in an industry where that kind of behavior is more predictable, as I've learned through the years.

I went for an AIDS test for approximately four months steadily afterward. This was within my first two months of living in DC. And it was the height of the AIDS scare. The word back then was that it had a ten-year incubation period. So I marked that date on my calendar. I was scared to death.

To this day I never found out if this was that singer's MO—to rape unsuspecting young girls. And I never shared the experience with anyone—I was too embarrassed. I thought people might have said that I asked for it. What was I doing in his hotel room? And checking my background more, "Oh, yeah, and you're a cokehead!" Yes, a naïve cokehead—but a cokehead all the same. So I couldn't tell anyone. I didn't even share it with the woman at the clinic, where I went for my AIDS tests and a pregnancy test. The clinic was all I could afford on nine thousand dollars a year. And I went there every month religiously after the rape. Pregnancy? I didn't trust the drugstore, I wanted a professional test.

I had insurance but was too scared that everything would be traced back to my job. I wanted to take the test because I wanted to know what my next move would be. If I was pregnant, I needed to make plans. And if I had AIDS, I needed to make plans. I would be done with the radio career. I would move back to Jersey because I would have wanted to be protected from the devastation mentally, first of all, that having AIDS would have done to me.

And physically, the ravages that you saw with the earlier pictures of AIDS made me know I needed to be around people who loved me. And I was still under the age of twenty-five and technically speaking, still under my parents' insurance, tax paying and all that. I knew I could go home to my parents. I would never have told them exactly how I contracted the disease—I would not have told them I had gotten it from being raped. I had a story all ready for them, just in case. One thing that everybody knew is that you didn't have to keep fucking to get AIDS. And I'm in the crazy entertainment business. Heck, it would have been easy to explain that I got with one of these dirty industry muthafuckas and caught the virus.

I would have just quit the business and gotten a quiet, low-key job in Monmouth County. I would have lived in my bedroom at my parents and just waited for the sickness to blow up. I would have at least had proper insurance coverage and someone to confide in as I was going through it. It wouldn't have been friends. And as far as relationships, I already lived a life of celibacy so it would not have been difficult to keep that up. When I was in the Virgin Islands I became the master of self-pleasure. That worked very well for me.

After I left the clinic the day after the rape I stopped off at my connection's place and picked up a package. And after snorting cocaine for most of the afternoon, I finally picked up the phone and called my father. I was in a coke stupor, which makes you very talkative. I rambled on about how I loved him and Mommy and how entertainment is really something else. I asked him how they were doing. And I started crying.

I think that while my father had no idea why I was really calling he got this much out of the conversation: "This is my baby girl and she misses home very much and is feeling lonely." I couldn't tell him that it was only part of the truth.

It wasn't unusual for me to call on a Saturday night. They would never think, "Hmm, why isn't she out, something must be wrong," because they knew I hardly ever went out. I've always been a sort of solitary person who didn't hang out much in the streets.

When I went to work the next Monday, Neville, who was also one of my party buddies, asked, "How was your date with Mr. X? You know that nigga's nasty. Yeah, he just got out of jail. Girl, you were in way over your head." And I thought, "Why the hell didn't you tell me this shit *before* I went out with him?" and I also thought, "Damn! Jail!"

And all these images ran through my head. You know what goes on in jail. (You watched *Oz!*) I became really paranoid. Then I started rationalizing. "Well, he's too big so I know he wasn't taking it; he had to be giving it." But then I thought, "But he's a real pretty muthafucka." I was just a mess.

Eventually I stopped taking the AIDS test. Along the way I got false information and found out that taking the test every month was futile. The disease can live dormant in your system anywhere from three to ten years. So I said to myself, "Fuck it! If I got it, I got it. I can't live being afraid." But what this did was make me even more isolated. And it drove me even deeper into my cocaine world. I started partying even harder—me and the white lady, cocaine.

There were plenty of industry parties in DC, the Chocolate City. And all of a sudden for the first time in my life I was actually becoming a fixture at these parties. Yes, I was at the industry parties, which I was able to attend because my program director was young and also trying to be known in the business and he dragged me along with him. We all aspired to be part of FM radio. Being at these parties gave us a taste of that life.

Soon I started to be noticed—not because I worked at an oldies station (AM at that) but because I was this cute girl at the parties. My looks were starting to get me invited to parties without people knowing who I was. It was at one of these parties where I met my cocaine connection via somebody who I had met in DC. During this time in DC, I was copping off the block or taking one-on-ones from party people. But once I met my connection, I was then able to stop having to ask, "Can I get in on your package?" because I knew I liked it enough to get my own.

My connection and I got along right from the start in that very feminine way (*How you doin'?!*). He seemed like a regular guy. He had salt and pepper hair, he spoke correct English and was very nonthreatening. He wasn't sexually threatening to me and I wasn't legally threatening to him. Once we were comfortable with each other, he gave me his address and I would go by his house several times a week and sniff cocaine from the house chair, a La-Z-Boy. After I had snorted to my heart's content, I would purchase my package and leave. I would do from the house chair some nights for four hours. Sure, sure, sure. I would always pick up my own package and go about my business. At that point there was no paranoia. I would pick up my one gram about every other day or three times a week and be on my way.

I wasn't worried then about being spotted or seen—remember,

I wasn't famous and I wasn't really thinking about who knew me. And while I was doing my thing at my connection's home, sitting in his La-Z-Boy, the doorbell was ringing and people were coming and going. They may have given me a "What's up" before they took a few lines from the house tray, too, while sitting on the couch next to the La-Z-Boy (which I monopolized). Then they would get their shit and be on their way like it was no big deal.

His clientele had just as much to lose at that point as I did. They weren't entertainment folks. They were engineers, school-teachers, white-collar workers. This was not a scene from *The Corner* or anything. It was like hanging out at a friend's house and there just happened to be cocaine on the living room table. My dealer wasn't a thug or a gangster. He was a sophisticated, effeminate man with a nice apartment (that he owned), with nice furniture, a designer mirror (for cocaine, of course) and everything laid out for his respectable clientele.

Hanging at Andre's (not his real name) house was socializing, but it was socializing with the underworld. Everybody had above-board jobs but nobody talked about their jobs while they were there. If there was a teacher, I didn't know where the teacher taught. People kept their private lives private. No one knew who was married or who had children or who drove what car. We weren't there really to socialize. We were all there for one pur-pose—to get high.

My dealer, I mean, sophisticated supplier (doesn't dealer sound so dirty?), had the kind of clientele that made me very comfortable. This wasn't a gossipy cipher. Andre and I would talk but it wasn't gossip. And it was nice to know that I was doing my thing alongside doctors, lawyers, teachers and everyday, regular Joes. Once I had my own dealer I stopped going to industry parties. I did two things—stayed home doing cocaine and worked.

In addition to being my dealer, Andre was a friend. He probably would not have been a friend if I wasn't doing coke. But I was and birds of a feather tend to flock together. I invited him to go to my first radio convention in 1987. He drove with me from DC to Atlantic City to IMPACT, a music/radio convention.

I met Cool DJ Red Alert within my first few minutes of arriving. He was on an escalator going up, I was going down. I said, "Hi, DJ Red Alert!" And he said, "El La Poo Poo!" That was his signature saying. I was so excited.

I was with Andre and needless to say, I was fucked up. I brought him because he was somebody who knew the other side of me and also knew I was involved in radio. He accepted me. He was like my security blanket. I had never been to a convention and I could have someone to break the ice with me, and if I couldn't break the ice at least I'd have someone with whom I could sit in the corner and talk about people.

While walking through the convention I ran into another famous New York radio deejay—not a personality, but a person who actually spins records. We spoke. He was very nice. He happened to be hanging out with a very famous rapper at the time. Andre knew that both of these guys did coke heavily because he knew their DC supplier when they came to town on tours.

Andre starts in with the subtle drug talk and the next thing you know all four of us are in a hotel suite getting skied out of our minds.

The rapper was the first person I ever met who exemplified extreme paranoia due to cocaine abuse. I never met anyone who opened up closets, looked under beds, flipped the blinds. We couldn't order anything from room service because he was afraid that any knock on the door would be the cops. The rapper's behavior was really bizarre. Even being fuuucked up, I recognized that he was acting strange. I had not reached the point in my addiction to even understand paranoia (but I would).

Cocaine was all fun to me. And I was having loads of fun. I missed the whole convention because we met them practically when we got there. We were in that hotel room for two days straight. The rapper and the deejay would have groupies come to the suite and when they were done, the hootchies would leave via the bedroom door. There were girls coming and going.

We got high nonstop—snorting, cooking and smoking. We only took a break when we ran out of baking soda. Andre and I ran to the store at five o'clock in the morning to get some. We were on some sort of coke binge. It was crazy.

When we got back to DC, Andre and I were still hanging hard. One time he made a delivery to my home and he brought about five people with him. I guess it was a party of sorts, which was very rare for me. He brought people who I had seen before and was cool with. I never entertained in my apartment because I lived in a so-called ghetto on Sherman Avenue right near Howard University. I spent much of my time in my apartment—I would leave it, go to work and come back to it.

But I was okay with Andre showing up to my house for what turned out to be a coke party. We were all smoking and sniffing and having a merry old time. And everything was great until I passed out. This was the first time I had ever passed out. And when I came to, everybody was at the door with their coats on, like they needed to be out just in case I was dead or something. They would have left me there to die.

That was a lightbulb moment for me. Getting high with muthafuckas doesn't do anything for you except give people something to talk about or worse. Nobody's going to stick around if something does go down. And nobody's got your back. That's just that world. If somebody passed out in front of me, I would be out, too. I never blamed the cipher. I just learned an internal lesson: Don't believe that people are going to be there for you if you're doing something illegal or just plain ill. Your boys who you think are holding it down with you on the block or your girls who you think have your back, the second they get caught up in some shit don't think that they either won't actually be out or turn your ass in if pressed by the authorities. That's a reality.

I'm not just saying this because it happened to me. I watched it happen to Jayson Williams, the former NBA all-star. He has all of these people over his house—supposedly a bunch of his friends. And somehow a limo driver is found shot to death in Jayson's bedroom. At first no one knows what happened. Everybody says it was an accident and that the driver somehow shot himself. But when pressed, one by one, Jayson's friends turned on him. And now he's facing a trial and many years in jail. What happened to that limo driver was tragic and no one deserves to die, I'm just making a point that people who you think are down for you and have your back no matter can turn on you on a dime. The law has a way offering deals so sweet for people to turn against each other that eventually everybody folds like a cheap suit. Even Sammy "The Bull" Gravano folded. And that's the mob. So what could I possibly expect from some cokeheads I barely knew? Of course they would roll out. I would do the same. I don't know anybody who would have been there for me when I came to. They were just doing their thing. No hard feelings. But it began a period of real isolation and paranoia for me. No more coke parties at my place, that's for sure.

Certainly there would be no more sharing of my secret with people in the industry. At these little industry parties that I was going to, even though it seemed as though many people were doing cocaine, I also knew that I could never use my cocaine use as entré into the business. I knew I couldn't break into the business via doing coke. Just like I somehow knew it wouldn't be cool for me to break in via fucking. Sure I could have easily caught some deejay's eye or some big ballin' jock's eye and gotten down like that and ended up as his sidekick on a morning show. Or I could have been one of his "coke buddies." But somehow I knew those two ways of breaking into the business would be a big no-no.

CHAPTER 4

Me and the White Lady

I HAD BEEN WORKING AT WOL-AM for a couple of months and I was starting to settle into this radio game. Even though I was not at all a player yet, our station would still command enough respect for artists to come through on promotional visits. It was more out of respect to our owner, Kathy Hughes, who carried a big stick in DC.

My show was the only "new jack" type of show on the station. I would play five percent oldies and the rest of the music would be current hits. I played eight songs an hour—one would be "Strokin'" by Clarence Carter and the rest would be Heavy D, Whodini or Salt-N-Pepa.

Salt-N-Pepa had "Tramp" out at the time. They came to DC for a week to promote their album. Artists will have a press junket in a town and go from station to station. Salt-N-Pepa came by WOL early in the week during my show and I interviewed them. We really hit it off. In the middle of the week there was some industry party featuring Salt-N-Pepa. It was one of the rare parties I would attend because I was deep in the throes of cocaine and I didn't like to be around people when I was getting high.

The thing that lured me to the function was Salt-N-Pepa. I liked the girls, wanted to support them. By the end of the week Herby (Luvbug) Azor, their manager, called me.

"The girls really like you," he said. "Spinderella is leaving to get married and we all kind of agreed that you would make a great new Spinderella. What do you think?"

I don't remember it taking me longer than the beat of a heart before I said no thank you. I was very flattered. I was a nine-thousand-dollar-a-year jock and they were nine-thousand-dollar-a-year rappers, so my career and their career were on about the same level financially.

There was no way I was going to call my parents and say, "Guess what, I'm joining a rap group!" You must be crazy. It was bad enough that I was working in radio. But after "four years of college!" to go off and become a deejay for a rap group, that would have sent them over the edge.

Rap music hadn't taken off at that point as far as being a respectable money-making vehicle. And they weren't the big Salt-N-Pepa that they became. They were brand-new and my radio career was brand-new. I just could not take a chance on something I really didn't know about and they knew that I was not a deejay, in terms of being able to spin records. But they told me that it was okay, that I would be able to fake it. It was all about the look.

At this time, I definitely had the look. I was Cocaine Wendy—about fifty pounds thinner than I was in college, model thin. My natural hair was not nearly as big as I wear it today, but it was pretty, long and a nice texture. And I've always been cute in the face. I was what they were looking for in a new Spinderella.

But I also knew that Cocaine Wendy wasn't the truth. Once I got myself together and gained that fifty pounds back the gig would be up. We would be on tour somewhere in Europe and while on tour I could see me packing on the pounds and by the end of the tour they would say, "You're not a good mixer and you gained all this gotdamn weight, go the hell back home!

Salt-N-Pepa also met Rock 'n' Roll Wendy—party girl. But I was really still Wendy from Wayside, who liked to be close to home. I knew that Wendy from Wayside was not going to Germany to stand on stage at some big rap concert. That wasn't where my heart is. I am my parents' daughter and I just knew that was not for me. I don't blame Salt-N-Pepa for that, I'm just saying the reason it took me only two seconds to say thank you so much, but no thank you.

I often think today what would have happened if I'd said yes. Can you see me in that "Shoop" video? No. Me neither. Dee Dee Roper was the perfect choice. And I think I made the right choice, too.

It wasn't but a few months after this offer that I got another that would change my career.

The call came on Halloween eve 1988. It was from the program director of HOT-103—the man I had begun hounding from the Virgin Islands and then from DC for the last year, sending him tapes every month and following up with calls. My persistence had finally paid off.

"So, do you still want to work in New York?" he said.

"Oh boy, golly gee, do I?!" I said. (Yeah, I think I said those exact words.)

The call came in around ten in the evening. Radio is a twenty-four-hour business, so that was not unusual.

"We have a situation here and I need you tomorrow night at midnight," he said.

"I'll be there," I said. No hesitation. I was going to be there. The next day I left very excited about finally making it to New York. The radio station was located in Astoria, Queens. I was very familiar with Manhattan because I used to go there frequently when I was growing up in Ocean Township. But I didn't know very much about the outer boroughs. And my dumb ass never bothered to ask, "Queens? Okay, how do I get to the station?"

I knew the address from sending them my air-check tapes every month. But knowing the address was absolutely no help. I got out of the Lincoln Tunnel and was lost after that. But I didn't panic. I had my friend, the white lady, traveling with me.

Please don't ask me how I had the nerve to drive two hundred miles up the New Jersey Turnpike to a brand-new job, a dream job, a dream about to come true with this bitch in the car with me. But I did. While driving on the New Jersey Turnpike with two to three grams of cocaine in my car was risky, for some reason I didn't think twice about it.

I was definitely on my way to becoming an addict but at this point I was still pretty much in control of my faculties. Using cocaine didn't make me more outgoing. I was already that. At the time I thought using it made me deeper. I felt like the white lady made me think deep thoughts. She helped me plan. With her, I felt as though I was always one step ahead of the next person. What my futuristic vision and self-imposed exile from society gave me naturally, the white lady took all of that to another level. Being high put me in my own zone. It made me feel as though I had one over on the world.

The world saw this goody-goody, nice girl with the nice upbringing. But inside I was a real bad ass. Cocaine gave me an edge that I now realize I never needed. Things at that time were about to happen for me that would have already given me that edge.

And working in New York, I knew I needed an edge—and a whole new image. I started getting my hair professionally weaved. In DC I wore my hair natural—which was basically in a mild Farrah Fawcett-like do. I fit in with the oldies, "buppie" look. This was a good look for DC Wendy. But New York Wendy needed something a little bit more dramatic. I wanted a look that said, "I'm here!" I wanted more, more, more of what I had. I knew I was only working one day a week in New York but I wanted them to notice me on my one day. I remembered the days as an intern on the morning show in Boston when I first learned that my personality and big nails could get me noticed and I applied the same rules here.

I was still working my afternoon shift in DC and doing overnights—midnight Sunday into five-thirty Monday morning. That's the shift where general managers try out new talent. It's the make or break shift. You'll find in any city whoever is on midnight Sunday into five-thirty on Monday morning is the person generally with the least amount of experience who is either trying to jump off or simply will never jump off and be relegated to that slot for their entire career.

If you are a radio head and you hear that a job is available at a station and you want to know what they're doing with that job, listen to that overnight shift Sunday into Monday morning. You'll hear someone new every week because they're trying people out for that open spot. That was the shift I was offered. I had to join the union, American Federation of Television and Radio Arts (AFTRA), and scale pay for a shift at that time was a hundred and five dollars. I had just gotten a raise in DC from nine thousand to eleven thousand a year. Now I was adding to the hundred and five, plus whatever money I made on appearances, which was no less than four hundred and fifty per appearance. I felt like I was moving into the big leagues.

I was finally in New York. I was at HOT-103 where the legendary Al Bandero did afternoons and the legendary Freddie Colon did nights. Bandero and Colon? You better recognize! This was big. When I was in college, I used to drive to New York, just to listen to New York radio stars like Bandero, Colon, Frankie

Crocker and Carol Ford. I needed to know what they were doing, how they were doing it and learn from them. Bandero did a weekend shift that led into mine. I would often get to the studio early and sit and talk with him. I was already excited to be talking to him and the coke I was on made me really talkative. Thinking back, Bandero must have known what was up. Excessive talking. That was a classic sign of being high on coke and he had been around. I was talking away, all wide-eyed, which I am already naturally. Can imagine how bugged out my eyes must have been when I was high. Wide-eyed and talkative. I'm sure Bandero enjoyed the company and I'm also sure he was thinking, "This bitch is high."

I was enjoying my jump-off, though. I was very happy to be working there. I was the only black on the staff—which is one of the reasons why they hired me. They didn't come out and say it, but I knew the deal. I was just black enough to represent black without being a real "sistah" to them. I was black but I didn't threaten the pH balance of the Debbie Gibsons and the Pretty Poisons and Paula Abduls. I was black the way Downtown Julie Brown—who was one of the hottest VJs on MTV at the time—was black. And I didn't mind that at all because Downtown Julie Brown was doing okay for herself. I would not have minded following in her footsteps.

I would leave DC either Sunday morning or Sunday afternoon or Saturday if I had an appearance on Saturday in New York. And I was always on time. I prepared for anything and everything.

One time I left a little later than usual. And when I got to the approach of the Lincoln Tunnel, traffic was backed up and not moving at all. I figured there was an accident inside the tubes. I didn't wait around to find out what the problem was. I parked my car on the side and called Triple A to tow it. I got out of my car and I walked through the Lincoln Tunnel. When I got inside I realized there was indeed an accident and I acted like my car was part of the accident and just walked right on through. I caught a cab on the other side to the station and I still wasn't late. I was committed.

I understood the importance of being reliable and showing up. So after I did my New York shift, I would turn around, hit the road and make it to DC in time for my regular shift there. I never missed a shift.

Sometimes, I would even hang around in the HOT-103 studio after I got off at five-thirty. I was still into the wonderment of it all being in New York and sometimes I would sit in the jock lounge for two hours, thinking, "Wow! I'm here!" I would just sit there looking at names on the boxes. "Wow, Al Bandero's jock box. Wendy Williams's jock box. Wow!" Station memos! I would save everything with HOT-103 on it that would be addressed to "staff." I was staff. I was so excited. I would do the appearances on the weekends that other jocks would turn down.

Sometimes two hours would turn into three hours because of the white lady. I would be back and forth to the bathroom and then I would just sit there until the high was over so I could have a clean drive home. It was crazy.

The drive home took about five hours. I would listen to

Howard Stern most of the ride. Thank God for syndication. When I crossed that imaginary line from New York into the South Jersey/Philly area, Howard would be on, still on the same joke. Then I'd cross into the Baltimore area and there was Howard Stern. He was still on when I reached DC. It was one big thread. And even though my parents lived along my route, I never stopped home. I never called any friends.

First of all, my friends only listened to KISS and WBLS. They were not up on dance music. So I didn't tell any of them about my new job because I was about to make my jump-off and I didn't really want anyone coming around with any of their thoughts. And in addition to becoming a potential star, I also had this habit, this secret that very few people knew about. And even though I had met schoolteachers and all like that who also used, their intake wasn't what mine had become. I used two grams a day, four days a week. And that habit was getting bigger with each trip down the highway.

Sometimes I would catch a nap on the road at the rest stops, where I would get some food, too. I knew I would have gotten a better meal at my parents' house and definitely a better nap but I still never stopped. See, they were part of the naysayers. They were the ones thinking, "Oh, this entertainment business! Why doesn't she just go and get a *real* job, already?"

I figured if you weren't going to be about my struggle, you didn't need to know anything about my struggle. In addition, if you wanted to be always checking my eyes because you thought this whole rock 'n' roll thing is nothing more than booze, drugs and sex, then you were going to find what you were looking for—which is that I'm fucked up. I am really fuuuucked up.

So I became a turnpike expert. I have stopped at every rest stop along I-95 from Molly Pitcher to the Maryland House. I can tell you which rest stops are the most comfortable, which has the best food and the cleanest rest rooms. I can tell you within each stop the best areas to sleep. I can even tell you the best angle to face your car if you go to sleep at six in the morning so that sun is not blazing in your face if you wake up at nine. I even knew what time the cleanup men came around to sweep up cigarette butts.

I kept a quilt, a pillow and a clean pillow case and an alarm clock in my car at all times. I had baby shields on the windows of my Subaru. And when I got tired I would stop at a rest stop, set my alarm clock and get my thing on with the white lady. (If there was any left. Oftentimes my package would be finished by four in the morning.) And when I got tired, I pulled off and I slept.

I didn't have to report to work in DC until three in the afternoon and I could pretty much do that show in my sleep. It wasn't about gossip and sharing insider dirt back then, so I didn't need any preparation. The music was laid out and I just had to do the breaks and the intros. I would often go in right off the road, unshowered. When I got home at seven-fifteen, I would take my shower and go to bed and get up to work my regular shift the next day at three. I loved my schedule.

A month after working at HOT, the station moved to 1372 Broadway in Manhattan from Astoria, Queens, where the *Cosby*

Show was taping and where sports station WFAN is still today. They moved and changed frequencies to 97.1 to become HOT-97. It was a stronger signal than 103, which means more people could hear them clearly. They were still doing dance music at the time. And I was doing more and more appearances.

During these days the radio station always provided transportation to your appearances. And HOT always did it with style. I would drive into the city to the station and I would be met by a stretch limo. The limo would take me to the appearance and drop me back off at the station afterward. I felt like a celebrity myself.

For four hundred and fifty bucks all I had to do was go to some club, get on the mike for a few minutes and say, "Hey! Ho! Is Brooklyn in the house?!" I would hang out for two hours in the VIP section drinking champagne and then go home or ego to the next club. I often had two appearances a night. In New York City there are so many clubs and so few jocks to do club appearances. The money was great—I'm was traveling by limo, drinking champagne, the toast of the party. It was very intoxicating. I wasn't jaded back then. I was wide-eyed and excited. And clubs weren't dangerous at all. They were places to have fun. I was beginning to have a little too much fun.

My cocaine habit was getting deeper. My packages for the road were increasing. I had to stockpile for that one night in New York. That was like the longest shift in the world. This routine went on for about three months. For about three months I drove up and down the turnpike—me, Howard Stern and the white lady, who was beginning to take a more active role in my life. I had been getting high in the studio my whole career. I smoked weed at WRBB in college, smoked weed in St. Croix, dabbled in coke in DC and now by my second month at HOT I was not only transporting large quantities of cocaine with me on my trips, I was actually getting high in the studio while on the air. I even developed a routine. By about two in the morning after I settled into my shift, I would take a break. There was a song called "Silent Morning" by Noel that was eleven minutes long. This gave me plenty of time to go to the ladies room, take a couple of hits and be nice and high for a couple of hours.

I might take one shorter break later. I tried to save some for my five-hour drive back to DC. If I was getting high on the road, I would pull off frequently. At this point, I was into cooking cocaine and found my best high came from smoking it off a stem. You can't really smoke cocaine off a stem and drive at the same time—or at least I hadn't quite mastered the technique. Besides, I wanted to enjoy my high.

I couldn't go to rest stops to get high because they were too well lit and I did not have tinted windows. So I had to go to spots where a lot of people were hanging out and I wouldn't be noticed. I would sit in my car, which was a mess, and smoke. When you get high the way I was getting high, you get sloppy with a lot of things. It was a chore for me to take a shower and feather my hair most days. Clean my car? Pu-lease! And I wasn't trying to leave my car anywhere to get it tinted because I didn't want folks peeping my sloppiness and I was too deep in my love affair with the white lady to actually clean it myself. So I had window shields—the baby pull downs. And I would pull over, pull down my shades, and take out my shit and my stem—which was about twice the circumference of a straw and half the length. At one end of the stem I would put a screen, in which I used a little cigarette ash to catch some of the moisture and I would pull my rock right off the spoon with a toothpick, put it in the screen and be on my way. And I knew how to whip it up so that it would be a nice chunk, too. My boyfriend in college introduced me to cooking it. He would do it for me when we smoked cocaine, which was very rare. But Andre, my dealer in DC, made me an expert.

I never smoked in the studio—even though I could because hardly no one was in at that hour. Cooked cocaine has a distinct smell. I never wanted it wafting into the hallway, giving me away. My routine was always to put on the Noel extended-play record and do my thing, come back and work out my shift, high as a kite.

On one particular night, I put on Noel, went to the ladies room, which was always empty because I was the only lady there during the midnight to five-thirty shift. I got my spoon and lighter, stem and screen together, cooked my package and took a hit. I don't know whether the pull was too strong or whether the shit was just that pure but it hit the back of my head like a sledgehammer and I passed the fuck out. I fell down. I must have fallen forward onto the heating register on the wall because when I came to *it* and *me* were on the floor.

Oh shit! Oh shit! Oh shit! How long have I been on this floor? And what the fuck is the heating register doing on the floor next to me?

Those were the only thoughts running through my head as I lay on the floor of the bathroom. When I finally got up and back into the studio, the phones were ringing off the hook and there was dead air—that Noel song had long played out and there was nothing in the studio but silence. The station had dead air for more than three minutes while I was unconscious. In radio, dead air for even seconds could get you fired. So three minutes of dead air?! Well, you know.

I got up and went back into the studio and there was no caller ID back then, so I couldn't tell who was calling. I was hoping it wasn't any of my bosses. A lot of listeners were calling and asking what happened. I told them that I had to go to the bathroom, that I had taken a whole lot of Correctol.

"You can't believe what that mess did to me," I told everyone who called me. "And they don't leave me up here with anyone to press the next song. Sorry."

It was believable. Believable enough that if any of the bosses called, they would have gotten the same story. Other jocks had been complaining about the station getting an instant-fire cart machine so when one song ends, the next one plays automatically. But what the bosses always felt about that was that it would make the jocks lazy. You would be able to walk out of the studio and have the show run itself and they were right, to a degree. But if I had an instant-fire cart machine no one would have been the wiser.

With each call I took I kept an eye on the hot line—a direct line used by the bosses into the studio. I was nervous waiting for it to ring. I waited fifteen minutes and there was no hot line call. I waited thirty minutes, no hot line call. I was in the clear. I had gotten away with it. And instead of the close call making me want to stop, getting away with it gave me even more courage to continue.

For me it wasn't about getting high—the excitement and the pleasure came from the process of getting high. If I could just take a pill and experience the high of being on cocaine, I wouldn't be interested in getting high. I enjoyed the process of bringing the straw to my nose. I enjoyed the process of breaking the rocks, cooking it up on a spoon and getting that first pull. I'm sure it's that way with weed smokers. The process of clearing the seeds, splitting the cigar to make a blunt or rolling a joint is just as much a part of the high as smoking the weed itself.

Somehow in the midst of all of this cocaine use, I got offered a full-time job at HOT working the overnight shift Monday through Friday, and I had to make a decision to leave DC. I had a problem: How would I get my coke? Yes, that was a bigger problem than quitting my job in DC and taking this new job, which was paying AFTRA wages in the ballpark of forty thousand a year. I knew I couldn't drive down to DC and get enough to last me until I could drive down again. Hell, if I did that, I might as well be trafficking drugs.

During one of my appearances for HOT, I met a security guard at one of the clubs who also did work for the station. He was hitting on me. I wasn't feeling him in that way but we struck up a conversation. While he didn't pursue the pickup, he must have seen something in my eyes because somehow the conversation got around to cocaine. He let me know that he could get me whatever I needed. He did security at HOT and also had a drug business on Jerome Avenue in the Bronx. He said he would make "house calls" to the station whenever I needed.

My new dealer would make "food" runs for me during my shift. He'd come back with a bag of McDonald's. Hot Mickey D's fries would be on the top and my little white package would be lying low on the bottom of the bag. I would usually give the fries away because I had absolutely no interest in eating. Just as mouths water at the smell of hot McDonald's fries, my mouth watered at the thought of what was under those fries. When he would show up with that bag, my jaw would start to wind and for some reason I would have to go to the bathroom and have a bowel movement immediately. This feeling would be consistent until I quit the habit. This reaction would take over. After my bowel movement I had to have a hit. I was a full-blown addict—a full-blown addict with a dealer who made deliveries.

It had been six months of driving back and forth from DC to New York and that was finally going to end. When I got back to DC after the job offer, I typed up my letter of resignation, giving WOL two weeks' notice. I gave it to my boss at the time, Diana Williams. That was the proper and professional way, I thought, to handle it. Diana Williams told me, "Don't bother with the two weeks' notice." She basically told me to get the fuck out right then. She was very nasty and I was a little hurt. I had been a con-summate professional my entire time in DC. I never missed a shift and I represented the station well (as far as they knew). The way

Diana Williams handled that situation was very typical of the business, sad to say.

I soon got over my hurt. I was in the Big Apple. I was single, no kids, making more than forty thousand dollars a year, plus four-fifty for every appearance. I had no student loans, no car loans. And I had my cocaine. Life was perfect.

CHAPTER 5

Queen of New York

THE BOSSES AT HOT CALLED ME and told me to come in early. I took New Jersey Transit from my parents' house. I had no idea what they wanted. It was very unusual for them to call me early, especially knowing that I had to do an overnight shift that night. But I came, no questions asked. When I got there I walked into the general manager's office and one of his flunkies informed me that I was fired. They didn't give me a reason. And once again I was forced to accept how unpredictable and crazy my business is.

They didn't give me a reason and they didn't have to, unless you're a big player. And there was a clear difference between me and Al Bandero, who was a big player. I was making AFTRA scale; he was working on a major six-figure contract. Once again, I had no recourse. I tried to fight back the tears. I didn't want these muthafuckas to get that. But I couldn't help it. They started flowing. I cried right there in the office and asked one of the dumbest questions that has ever come out of my mouth: "Well, what am I going to do now?"

"I don't know, go get married and have some babies," the flunky said. He didn't say something reasonable, like go to another city and work someplace else for a while and try to come back. No, he said get married and have some babies! That pissed me off even more.

I collected my stuff, with my shoulders heaving from crying. Not one person came over and patted me on the back or tried to comfort me. I was never the kind of employee who people felt connected to. I was very standoffish and didn't extend myself. Not because I didn't like people—I love people—it's just that I didn't want to form any radio relationships because when shit is going good, you don't have any friends and when shit is going bad you don't need anyone pitying you.

Because I was only making union scale, there was no contract to break and no paperwork to fill out. I was just fired. Good-bye. But not having a contract worked in my favor, too. They couldn't stop me from getting a job at a New York station that next hour if I could. If I had a contract and was fired, they often write in non-competes preventing you from working in the area for a period of time. I had no such restrictions. After collecting my shit, I hopped a train to a friend's apartment in Newark and started working the phones.

I had been a part of the New York radio scene for two years. Surely somebody would want to hire me. After making a few calls, I found out that there was an opening at WPLJ. I called the station and the program director asked me to come in. He was familiar with my work at HOT and offered me the evening shift from ten to two in the morning. I was coming off overnights and slowly moving toward making a name for myself. The woman who had the shift, Linda NRG, was being moved to the morning team. That was the summer of 1989. I was happy at WPLJ, but I knew there were bigger fish to fry.

One August day I was walking down the street heading to the station and I bumped into Bugsy, a popular jock on WBLS. To this day, Bugsy is one of the most gracious, most well-versed people in the business that I know. He told me he was a fan of mine and that I was making quite a name for myself. He also told me that Tony Grey, program director at KISS-FM, was also a fan of mine. I was very flattered and honored. Bugsy and Tony Grey were in urban radio—the pinnacle to me. I was in "white" radio. And they still knew what I was doing.

I wasn't going to urban radio parties. I was busy hosting parties for white radio. White radio and black radio don't mix. The industry is small but the lines are drawn and they are definitive. But if you are black on white radio, people will know you. I should have gone to some of the urban radio parties, just to get my face out there. And it would not have been unusual at all for me to be there. While everybody was out partying, I was working, and during the day I was sleeping and in between it all I had a cocaine habit, which I was desperately trying to keep a secret. But in the midst of all of that, I still managed to cross over.

Tony Grey was a fan!

I called Tony Grey the next week. He surprisingly already knew I was working at 'PLJ. I asked him if he had anything going on at KISS. He told me he only had part-time work, which meant I would be making a hundred and fifty-five a shift (AFTRA wages went up a bit), versus the fifty thousand I was now making at 'PLJ (not including appearance fees). But I took Tony's offer and said good-bye to 'PLJ.

Growing up in Ocean Township was a wonderful learning experience for me in several different ways. One way in particular—being forced to deal with so many white people, thereby learning what they really think of blacks. Working at HOT and 'PLJ wasn't just about working with the white people at the station, it was catering to a majority white fan base. Tony Grey presented me the opportunity to work for an urban station, playing the music I chose to listen to when I got in my car. He never promised me a full-time job. But I had come far enough in my career to have enough belief in myself that something would jump off.

I was still living at my parents' house and had no debt and only one expense—cocaine, which was relatively cheap. I could still take the chance and see what happened. I had done well by my money, too. This was before the bling-bling era and I wasn't tricking out my money on clothes and jewelry. This was back during the time when Madonna had a boutique in Macy's and when wearing ripped tee-shirts and jeans and rubber bands on your wrists were cool.

Taking this job at KISS on the surface seemed really crazy. For one, it was a station with established jocks under contract. How in the world would I ever get a shift? Let's be real, you count on getting ahead based on people fucking up their job. They had Carol Ford in the afternoon; I finally got to meet her in person and I gushed all over. She was very sweet. There was no way I was taking her spot. Chris Welch was doing middays. I wasn't taking his spot, either. Yvonne Mobley was doing nights. And Diana King, who had left WBLS to come to KISS, was the first option at fill-in. Not only did I not have a regular shift, I was backup to the backup.

I knew my old college schoolmate would get the first call whenever a jock called in sick or went on vacation. I was called next. Why would I take this job? Futuristic vision. I knew eventually, somehow I would get a shot.

In addition to working part-time at KISS, Diana also had a part-time job at Lane Bryant. And oftentimes when the station would call, she was at Lane Bryant and couldn't just up and leave on the spot. I, on the other hand, was *always* available. I had purchased a beeper when I was at HOT, which was only used by my bosses to page me if they needed me to fill in. No one else had that beeper number but my bosses. Upon being hired at KISS, I gave that number to my bosses there. If they needed me, I would be there. In fact, I was usually there anyway. Even though I didn't have a regular shift, I would come into the city from my parents' house every day, just in case. I would either sit in the jock lounge and read the *Daily News* or go shopping. But I didn't want to be too far if they needed me to fill in. And as it turned out, I was filling in a lot.

About a week after I was hired, Tony Grey, my fan, left the station. They promoted the music director, Vinny Brown, into his spot. Vinny had been a jock in a small town down south somewhere before coming to New York. And now he was thrust into the big time, overseeing KISS. He was new, I was new and we hit it off. He loved that he could rely on me. And when I filled in for anyone, not only was I as good as the jock I was replacing, in many cases, I was even better.

KISS and WBLS were the only urban stations in town. And 'BLS in an attempt to take the top spot, started stealing a lot of talent from KISS. They stole Mike Love, our morning man. And they were coming after anyone not under contract. The ground was rumbling. KISS, knowing I wasn't under contract, did not want to lose me to WBLS. They formulated a new morning show featuring Ken Webb and Jeff Fox and they brought me on full-time—it was called *The Kiss Wake-up Club*. They locked me into a contract and I would do the traffic and *Dish the Dirt,* a segment I invented. KISS canceled the official traffic service and I would call in and get the traffic and report it every ten minutes. I wasn't trained to do traffic, but I was flattered that KISS wanted to save me. I was trained in dishing the dirt, though. That was the early version of what I'm most known for today. I would read the papers and report the dealings of celebrities, and I would go to the parties and do my celebrity spottings and let the audience know what was going on at the parties, too.

In addition to my spot on the *Wake-up Club,* I became the official spokesperson for NutriSystem. They were one of the station's biggest advertisers and I got a nice paycheck to do a few spots for them every day. This was a way for me to keep my voice and name out there during the entire day. A couple of spots would run on each shift.

I would ad-lib for sixty seconds, telling everyone how wonderful NutriSystem was.

"Hi, everybody! This is Wendy Williams for NutriSystem . . ." and I would proceed to tell them about my fat bubbling over on the train and how much I appreciated the job NutriSystem was doing on my body. At this point the weight loss I had experienced from my coke diet had long since worn off. I was definitely pushing two hundred pounds, making me the perfect spokesperson for NutriSystem.

"Hi, everybody! This is Wendy Williams for NutriSystem. The holidays are here and my mother's cooking. But I'm on NutriSystem. They have these turkey patties. You pull out the hot sauce and get you a piece of lettuce and you can enjoy the holidays without missing out on a delicious meal . . ."

After one year on the *Wake-up Club,* Vinny gave me my own shift—six to ten in the evening. Diana was very pissed. She had gotten to New York first. She was Frankie Crocker's fill-in. She had gotten to KISS before me. When 'BLS was stealing people they didn't offer her a contract, they gave it to me. And now I was getting a shift while she was still doing fill-ins.

It was the latter part of 1990 and I was being paid sixty thousand, plus appearances, plus NutriSystem money. I expanded my *Dishing the Dirt* to my night show where celebrities would frequent the studio for interviews and I developed my style of high drama and scandalosity. I was having a ball.

My coke connection from HOT followed me to KISS. He was no longer working for HOT but he always had a side job in addition to dealing coke. He would be doing security someplace and dealing coke. He would be driving a truck and dealing coke. He would be working for UPS and dealing coke. I'm doing nights at KISS and I'm up to my same old coke tricks. But it's getting more difficult to hide because people are starting to know who I am. When I was on appearances for HOT and 'PLJ, I could slip into the bathroom and take care of my habit, check my nose in the mirror and keep on partying. But now, when I go into a stall, I am followed by chicks who have heard me on the radio and know who I am.

I would get a tap on the stall and someone might say, "Wendy, you were talking about Aaron Hall's baby's mama the other day. Well, my girl here was dealing with Aaron and she has more stuff to tell you. Sheila! Get over and tell Wendy what's going on with you and Aaron Hall!"

Meanwhile I'm hunched over the seat with my coke and a straw doing a one-on-one—where you take a hit to one nostril and then a hit to another. *Bang, bang. What a rush!*

At the white stations on appearances the girls in the bathroom were polite and would say hello, but no one was banging on my stall trying to talk to me. By the time I got out of the stall, the bathroom is now full of women wanting to tell me something or say hello. All I wanted to do was get my hits on, check my nose and get the fuck out of the bathroom. But now I am forced to deal with the public in a way I had never imagined.

I'm trying to get high but I'm also trying to build what I hoped was a long career in radio and that meant paying attention to the listeners. Every listener counts, particularly in the jump-off stage. This was becoming a difficult balancing act for me.

These girls know the score. They know what a cokehead looks like. You could always play it off being high in a club. You could play it off like you're drunk (which was acceptable). But the way I was using, it would eventually become very hard to hide what I was up to. It became such a problem that I would get high as much as I could before my appearances so that I wouldn't have to take a bathroom break.

We'd pull up to a club—and at this time I was rolling with Skeletor, my assistant and Bulge, my security. I would send the fellows in to scope out the club and make sure the money was right while I'd sit in the car and sniff coke until they came back. No one knew what I was up to. Neither Skel nor Bulge indulged.

I kept my balancing act going. But I was becoming bigger and bigger on the air. There were articles written about me. In 1993 I was named *Billboard* magazine's "Radio Personality of the Year." I was in the spotlight. I had become "That Girl." I was talking that shit that everybody wanted to hear.

On the radio, I was becoming Queen of New York.

CHAPTER 6

Hey, Deejay!

WHILE I WAS DANCING with the white lady, I really didn't have time to dance with anyone else. I wasn't thinking about sex or dating or anything. I spent all of my time plotting on the next time I would get high and how. Instead of thinking about dating my main concerns were: Am I going to slice my lines with a matchbook or a razor? And what kind of mirror was I going to use? Which spoon would I use to cook it? How many lighters did I need for my session or should I use a butane torch? (You can get calluses using lighters too often.) How many cigarettes would I need to smoke to make the appropriate amount of ashes for my sessions? (When I cooked coke, I used a layer of ashes as a filter.) My main social activity was preparing to get high, getting high, coming down from my high and plotting my next time to get high.

Getting high became like my second job because when I was using cocaine at this point, I would get really lazy. I was so lazy that I started leaving bottles of water in the freezer when I was sober because once I was high, I knew I would be too lazy to pour water into a glass. I would even plot on what I would wear—my high gear—because I knew I would be too lazy to change, so I had to have on clothes comfortable enough to sleep in and clean looking enough to perhaps wear to work the next day because sometimes I would be too lazy to change my clothes for work.

I didn't have time for men and relationships at the height of my addiction. But somehow one managed to work his way in. I heard through the grapevine that this very popular deejay—one half of a famous deejay-rap duo—thought I was very cute and wanted to get to know me. I was very familiar with him. His group was legendary. He had somewhat of a juice card, which kind of turned me on. I really wasn't thinking about him having a lot of money and all that. Money was never a motivating factor for me.

It was 1990 and I was living in a one-bedroom apartment that had mice. But I had a housekeeper. It was a heavily Hispanic neighborhood on Washington Avenue in Union City. I was renting from people who were actually listeners of mine, I later found out. I must say, when I found out that the person I was renting from was a listener, I was a little embarrassed. I mean she knew how I was really living. I totally understand why rappers front a certain image to the world because when people listen and they realize what your actual deal is, there is a big letdown for the fan. The woman I was renting from owned the apartment and moved to a bigger place after she got married. I found her place advertised in the newspapers and got it immediately. I know she was telling her friends, "I'm renting to Wendy Williams!" There were many people who still remembered me from my days at HOT.

I had just started working at KISS doing the night shift. And coupled with the appearances I may have had after my shift, the hours were getting a little too hectic to be driving about an hour each way up and down the highway from New York to my parents' house every night. So I moved to Union City, which was a ten-minute ride to the city. The apartment had mice but it also had all of the amenities I needed, including a washer and dryer inside the unit. And it gave me the privacy I needed to continue my habit in peace. It also gave me the freedom to date—if I ever found spare time between work and this coke thing.

The deejay (we'll call him Johnny T) gave me reason to find some time for him. I met him at KISS. I was interviewing him about a hit song he had done on a movie soundtrack. He went out of his way to introduce himself to me. I found him to be very nice and charming. He was as good looking in person as he was on the album cover. More importantly, he was a perfect body match for me. I preferred a big man—a man who could handle me. (I still do.)

On our first date he picked me up in a truck—piped out, rapper style, with the rims and all the whistles and the bells. But little did I know that he didn't have money like that. It was all a front. And I was so naïve back then. I think even in my own fame, I probably was a bit of a groupie and impressed with all of the bells and whistles. I wasn't used to wearing my own badge of fame yet. I guess I looked at him as someone who would validate my fame, give me cachet. And I guess I brought something to the table for him, too—he was dating Wendy from the radio.

We didn't have a lot in common socially. He didn't drink. He didn't smoke weed. He didn't even use a lot of foul language. He definitely didn't do coke. In fact, I never dated a man with a habit.

In a strange way, being with me brought him more sophistication. We became intimate. He made me feel that it would be okay, like he would protect me. Johnny T's status was way bigger than the R&B singer who raped me. And despite all my fears I allowed him to have sex with me without wearing a condom. (I hear he is now dating an author and I'm sure not wearing condoms with her either because leopards don't change their spots . . . but that's another story for another day.)

Johnny T was very private. He only gave me his pager number but I didn't think anything of it at the time because, well, I was dating a famous deejay and he was with me—who cares about a number? And besides, I was too caught up in my own shit to notice that there's really something strange about being in a "relationship" with a man who you can only reach through his pager.

At this point my life was wonderful. Doing the night shift was great because I got to meet everyone—all of the big artists were now making the rounds to my show as well. And I didn't quite realize my own impact because I lived in a bubble. I would go in my bubble at the studio. And when I was home I had my habit. My habit was everything outside of the studio and any appearances I made for the station were one big blur. The appearances became for me just a place where I would pick up extra money to get back to my habit. I never dwelled in the VIP areas drinking champagne or socializing. I didn't have time for that—I had a package waiting for me.

But my fog was lifting, temporarily. I didn't mind bringing attention to myself at this point. I was dating a famous deejay, a man who was sober. And it was okay to be seen because my habit was "under control," or so I thought.

I started to enjoy my celebrity. I enjoyed everything about being involved with someone who was "famous." I loved the scene and at some point I thought that I could love him. But I never remember getting caught up in that, "Ooh, I love him," gushy, mushy sort of thing. And I know I didn't love him enough to stop my habit (he never even knew that I had a habit). Nor did I love him enough to press for a home phone number (dumb bitch that I was for allowing him to get away with that pager shit). Nor did I love him enough to bring him home. He was never worthy of family introductions. We all go through it, though. Some of us, unfortunately, don't ever snap out of it.

Looking back I was just one long, extended booty call for him. We didn't really have a relationship. It was all sex. The only time we really dated was at the very beginning of the relationship. Maybe we had eight dates during the course of that first year. Then it was him calling me at one or two o'clock in the morning to come over. That's a booty call, right?

Stranger things began to take place, like his truck would always be broken and in the shop. I started to realize things about him during my piques of sobriety. He didn't realize any of the things about me (like I was a cokehead) because he didn't really care about me. I was his booty call. And to make matters worse, the sex wasn't even that good. He never went down on me and when we had sex it was quick and without a condom. I must have been really high to allow that. Somewhere in my twisted mind I must have believed I was his only one and that he was really in the studio every night with his rap partner and that's why he came over so late.

He didn't smoke, he didn't drink and he rarely cursed and I guess I equated his behavior with being a "good" man. He ordered grapefruit juice all the time and I was just the one ordering the hard liquor and doing cocaine. But on the outside I was the nice girl from Wayside. And from the outside we looked like a great couple. He had his own apartment, which I never visited. When he wasn't with me, he was spending time with his daughter or in the studio, or so he said. When we were together his pager never went off—so it didn't appear that he had another woman or even his baby's mother hounding him. That's what I thought. So what, I wouldn't see him for two or three days? He was busy. And he would eventually always come around. At two in the morning he would call and tell me he was on his way. "Oh, it's been so hectic," he would say. "I'm coming over to see my baby."

Most of the time we would get right to the sex. I figured he had a lot of stress and it had been built up all day or three days since he had last seen me. We would have sex and I never had an orgasm. He doesn't eat pussy. Sex with him was not a pleasure but I didn't care because when he left I pleased myself, the way I had during my time in the Virgin Islands. For some reason I never really sweated it like that—having an orgasm during sex. (But believe me, I have since snapped out of that mindset. It is a *must* today.) Thinking back, how selfish was that on his part? But you know there will always be men like that as long as there are women like I was. It was all my fault for accepting that shit. I put up with it.

Being with him, I learned another valuable lesson: When you have sex—even bad sex, even sex without an orgasm—and you don't use a condom, you can get pregnant or worse. Yes, the trusty EPT test came back positive. And even in my cocaine haze it didn't take much for me to make the decision—hell, no, I wasn't having his baby.

At this point he had shown his true colors. He had borrowed money—under the guise it was for a birthday present for his daughter. I realized, financially speaking, he was not all that he was cracked up to be and definitely not the kind of man I wanted to raise a child with. He borrowed the little Eagle Talon I bought with vanity plates that read, "Wendy." This was 1990 into 1991 and I thought it was a step up from the Subaru. And putting my name on the plates, well, that was really balling.

We had been dating about a year and now I'm pregnant. And this "relationship" is real shady. Not only did I only have a pager number but he wouldn't call back right away, not even if I put "911" after my number. Back then I was using 911 the way girls use it today—not for real emergencies. I was really being the dumb bitch. I was the dumb bitch on a few counts—first for accepting only booty calls and second for not using a condom and last for allowing myself to be a nothing in his life. I never met his mother or his daughter. I met a few of his friends because looking back I realized that he enjoyed being with "Wendy Williams." I wasn't on the radio talking about our relationship but it was nice for him to be around his friends with me.

People saw us out but he didn't want us to be on the radio about it because I guess that was an effort to shield the other bitches that he was fucking from the truth. No, I never saw us getting married because too many things started happening. He was borrowing my car more and more and would be driving around for hours, sometimes leaving me stranded. I'd be waiting and waiting and waiting, tapping my feet and looking at my watch, waiting for my ride to pick me up in my own damn car to either go to work or be picked up from work. I would often have to take cabs to or from work. And my dumb ass would never go off on him. When he finally did show up apologizing I would say, "That's okay, baby." *Let that shit happen today!*

He would always use the studio as the excuse and I would never suspect that it was anything other than that. His other thing would be that he had to pick up his daughter who I completely understood was his first love. When I got my car back I would never comb it for weave hairs or look for lipstick or anything like that. It just never crossed my mind.

Oh, and Mr. Trifling would not only show up frequently late with my car but would give it back to me practically on fumes, below "E." And what would I do? Tell him, "Well, all right you know you left me with a little bit of gas. So next time take the gas card and fill it up for me, baby. Okay?"

So I gave him the credit card. Finally, at one point I decided my car was being used too much and I rented him a car. He had no credit card to rent one himself. I'm cheap, so I wanted to rent him a car from one of those low-rent rental agencies but it would take a couple of days. He was demanding, "Baby, I need a car now!" he said. "There's a car rental place on Forty-third Street." This was near the station, right in the heart of Times Square. Read: This car cost an arm and a leg to rent.

My credit card still had a fucked-up interest rate that was about twenty-one percent. I might have had a fifteen-hundred-dollar limit because I screwed up my credit in college buying shit I didn't need and not paying it off on time (you know I didn't have a job back then). I hadn't had my big financial lightbulb moment at this point, which was my divorce. So I rented him a car for what was supposed to be three days but ended up being thirty days. No lie. He had used up the entire balance on my credit card. I could not remember one gift that he had given me. While I'm not the gift-receiving type, a little pair of silver hoops at Christmastime or a card or a rose would have been nice.

He was never available so I spent my time with my lovely family back in Wayside. I never second-guessed it because I always had my own family; and next to my own family at Christmas, a package would have been the next most important thing to me . . . then my job and then him.

After the thirtieth day with the car the rental agency started calling me like crazy. They threatened to call the cops and report the car stolen. Finally, Johnny T answered one of my "911" pages. I told him the cops now have the plate number so he needed to return the car. I had seen enough of a temper in this guy (and mind you, he didn't have a bad temper but I had seen enough) that I knew that he could flip on me. I was already putting two and two together that I was just a side piece—a booty call.

He returned the car with an attitude. I took it back to the rental agency and the bill was thousands of dollars. I was over my credit limit. He never gave me any money for the car. And I never paged him again. That was the way the relationship ended. He never called me again. And I realized what I was to him and had put him in a category. You live, you learn, you move on and get over it.

He did, however, leave me with a seed growing in my body. I had never been pregnant before in my life and didn't know what the hell I was going through. I decided to take the test because one evening while I was coming around the loop outside the Lincoln Tunnel on my way home and I had to pull over to vomit. My first thought was, "Oh, Lord, I'm pregnant!"

I knew what I wanted to do at that point. I knew that in New Jersey two signatures were needed for any type of an abortion. I had always been pro-choice. And while I had never been pregnant, I had always prepared for it. Don't ask me where I got this knowledge. I guess I read enough magazines and watched enough Lifetime to know things. And even through my cocaine haze I knew that I was too much of a catch for a guy that was a part of the rap culture, baby's mama drama and shady ways, to drop a seed in me and move on. *Pu-lease!*

I made my appointment at a clinic in Manhattan. I had a perfectly good GYN in New Jersey and good insurance but I did not want this information getting out. I was popular. I have always been paranoid and until this day I'm still very paranoid with medical records and things like that circulating around. So I made my appointment for an abortion at a clinic that I found in the Yellow Pages because I wasn't asking anyone for any references. I took the day off from work, took a cab to the city, filled out the paperwork and made it seem like my boyfriend was coming back to get me later. I had on a baseball cap pulled down low with no fake ponytail, no makeup, no nail tips and no jewelry. I was ready for surgery. I didn't give them my real name. Was I scared? No! I felt no connection to the baby, which was about six weeks into developing. I looked at it as a little lima bean. I didn't feel like it was my child; there was no emotional attachment to it or to the father at this point. Hell, I felt more connected to the coke that was waiting for me when I got home. And that was another factor with getting the abortion. I thought even if I stopped doing the coke right then, what affect would my previous use have on the baby? I didn't know under what circumstances the baby would be born—I was doing coke every single day. And he didn't know. When you see a deejay on a booty call it's not like you're waking up in the morning spooning each other. He was hitting the skins and scramming. If I was lucky, I might get a couple of phone calls during the day but those calls were always made in front of his boys so he could show off, show his control over me. Those conversations would go something like this: "I'll be by around two to pick up the car and I'll talk to you later when I get out of the studio whenever that is." Then he would get off the phone. I was probably the brunt of all kinds of jokes.

There was no way I was having his baby. I wanted every part of him expelled from my body. I did not tell a soul about the pregnancy or the abortion—especially not him. This was the kind of man who if he knew that I was pregnant would all of a sudden become righteous. And if he found out I had an abortion he would go around all hurt letting the hip-hop nation know what I had done to *him*. There was no doubt in my mind that he would have wanted me to keep the baby because he was a product of his environment and I was a catch, quite frankly. And for me to have his baby would have been some sort of feather in his cap.

I paid for the abortion with cash, honey. There would be no paper trail on this kid. I told the people at the clinic that my man was coming to pick me up and they didn't check. Right before the abortion they did an ultrasound to see if I was still pregnant and they asked me if I wanted to see. "No!" I said. When it was done, I felt nothing emotionally; I was numb. I woke up groggy, lined up next to a bunch of other people who had to have been taken care of in the clinic. I might have been the only well-paid, well-insured dumb bitch in there. When the grogginess wore off, I ate some crackers, drank some juice, took the elevator downstairs, got in a cab and went home. I never shed a tear. I never called the nigga back. And I never looked back.

I don't feel bad to this day because having that baby would not have been the right thing to do. And I never blamed my past actions on what I eventually went through trying to have a baby with the man I eventually fell in love with, a man who gives me orgasms and for whom I became his wife and who finally became the father of my child.

But that day was a long time coming with a lot of pain and heartache in between. But the experiences and that man were certainly worth the wait.

CHAPTER 7

First-Husband Blues

IT IS AN UNSPOKEN RULE in radio that jocks and salespeople don't mix. Jocks are the prima donnas who bring in the revenue and the salespeople are the plebes who are responsible for selling the jocks. In radio they don't ever want the salespeople to "bother" the jocks, the stars. Robert Morris III (not his real name) somehow subtly managed to break through. I noticed him immediately because of his size—six-three, about three hundred pounds. Solid, just the way I liked my men. He was dressed in a Brooks Brothers suit and had graying hair, which I also loved because it was a sign of maturity.

I bumped into him in the hallway. He knew immediately who I was and struck up a conversation. Before I went to the studio he said, "By the way, I have this appearance that client wants you to do." He would frequently tell me about appearance opportunities—which was a big no-no. That info was to be passed from the salespeople to management to the jock. But I didn't mind, I liked talking to him.

I could tell he was attracted to me. I could also tell that he probably would never ask me out. He was a little intimidated. I was a big deal in New York. I was in the top three in my time slot and was bringing a lot of revenue to the station. And I had a big mouth. When women are strong and carry an air of mystique sometimes the strongest men don't want to ask you out. I was a woman who was aware of myself. I could see he was attracted. So the next time he approached me about an appearance he said something like, "Are you busy Saturday?"

I said, "Yes, I'm going out with you. You're taking me to BBQs."

"Well, what about this appearance?" Robert said.

"We'll go to BBQs, and you come to the appearance with me. We'll call it a date."

And that was how it started. We dated silently for eight months before we announced our engagement.

Robert was exactly what I was looking for in a man at the time—he was older, nearly forty, more mature, more stable (or so I thought). He was big and attractive. His only problem was his jacked-up teeth. But I figured those could be fixed. He seemed to have a lot of confidence and he made me laugh. I was in my mid twenties, making about eighty thousand dollars a year, living in a small apartment in Union City that had rats and roaches. I had broken up with a famous deejay and had an abortion. I figured the only thing I hadn't done and perhaps the next phase of my life should be marriage.

For some reason I started to get very worried about my parents not being around for the important activities of my life, like me getting married. Not that they were sick or in poor health but my futuristic vision was seeing every possible scenario, albeit far in the future. I wanted my father to be able to walk me down the aisle. I would never forgive myself if something happened to my parents or if something happened to me and I wasn't able to fulfill this part of my dream. That's the way I was thinking then.

I had the perfect career, I was making lots of money, I was rising to the top of my game. I just felt that I had to complete my circle—which meant getting married and having a child. Maybe other girls at twenty-five or twenty-six were still in the struggle to get their career together. I was beyond that and ready for the next phase of my life.

Robert seemed like the perfect man to carry out my plan. He was a fraternity man, like my father and brother. He got along with my family and believed in all the things my family believed in. We both came from a two-parent household. He grew up in a well-respected Manhattan household and I was raised in a predominantly white neighborhood in Monmouth County, New Jersey. His parents were a lot like my parents—they were never wealthy, just always lived in the right places and sent their kids to the right schools; dressed the right way, ate at the right restaurants and vacationed at the right places. My family vacationed in Martha's Vineyard and his went to Sag Harbor. My family traveled to the Orient by plane and his went by the Orient Express. His parents and my parents would even get together and we all would have champagne and caviar. We made a nice picture.

He was a "nice picture," too. And even though I knew there was a disparaging difference in our incomes, I figured that it would be okay because the background checks were all right. I never thought I was too good to date down financially. Never, ever. Hell, I would date a plumber or cab driver. I was never checking for a man's wallet.

Robert, though, had the "right" package. He even wore custom-made shirts with his initials on the sleeves. He had the right education. He was a Morehouse man, which I found absolutely wonderful. I loved the thought of Morehouse and Atlanta—that bastion of black pride.

What attracted me to him—what kept me attracted is that we could talk about things other than radio stuff, like what Mary J Blige was up to. He was a cornball, which was fine with me. I was living a fast life. I liked the slow pace he brought to my life. I was in the hip-hop game but my values were still Wayside.

But there were some warning signs that I should have paid attention to. I didn't realize that my family thought something was wrong with a man of his age being so available, so unattached, never been married without children. They would throw things out there and I would think, "Oh, you guys are crazy!" I just wasn't trying to hear them. I didn't feel that Robert was a father-figure. I had a father, a very good father at that.

He also lived with his parents. But in New York you sometimes forgive things you would never forgive anywhere else, like people in their forties who don't have a driver's license. New York is expensive and he wasn't making any money; I understood him living with his parents.

So we got engaged. He asked me to marry him at one of his fraternity functions. He had already shown his boys the ring—the ring that I picked out. It was a cubic zirconia. He originally picked out a real diamond that he could afford but it was about the size of a pinhead. I had to tell him, "You know, honey, if we ever got married, I could not have a little, tiny stone in my ring." I was seeing the hip-hop game starting to form. People were wearing the leather medallions with Africa on them, but it was fast moving toward the "bling-bling." And I was Wendy from the radio. Even if I was wearing a leather Africa medallion and Cross Colors and Karl Kani, once I said I was getting married people would look at the engagement ring and think or say aloud, "How did you do?" Heck, even outside the hip-hop game women immediately look at your ring to see what your future husband is all about.

So I picked out a nice-sized, high-quality cubic zirconia, which he presented to me at the biggest fraternity function of the year—their winter ball. We got engaged and I called my parents from the hotel room we rented at the venue in Yonkers.

My parents seemed very happy. It took a year to plan the wedding. At that point I was making enough money where I was willing to pay for the wedding myself. I was raised to believe that the woman's parents paid for the wedding. But because my parents paid for my education in full, I had a lot of guilt. I wouldn't dare make them pay for the wedding. Besides, I had excess income. My rent was cheap, my car was paid for and my taste in clothes was cheap—Timberland, Carhartt, etc. Coke was relatively cheap, too—about thirty dollars a gram. I used about three grams a day four days a week. So I paid for the wedding and asked my mother to plan it. I'm a girly girl but I was never into the pomp and circumstance. Actually, things like the details involved with planning a wedding make me vomit.

My mom planned it; I told her I just wanted to get married in a place that wasn't common. But I wanted to get married at the Jersey Shore where I was raised and I wanted Reverend Matthews from the Second Baptist Church, the church I was raised in, to marry us. My mom did a fabulous job. She handled everything from soup to nuts—everything except write the checks. And it was perfect. His parents even paid for the honeymoon. The only thing he paid for was the ring, which was three hundred dollars. They sent us to Rio de Janeiro and we flew first class. Everything went off without a hitch . . . until we got on that honeymoon. We fought the entire time. He didn't like what I was wearing. Or he felt like I was wearing too much makeup. Or "What's up with your hair?" It was so petty. At one point I remember saying, "Well, I'm flying back home!"

When we got back home, everything was fine. We kissed and made up. We flew back to an apartment that we had picked out in Jersey City in the Newport Apartments because I didn't want us to move into my apartment. I wanted us to start fresh in *our* apartment. The place was in my name because I was making more money and I was the one with the credit history—which wasn't perfect but good enough to secure an apartment.

I never got the chance to fully unpack before the fighting began again. We would fight about my hair. He liked it natural and I wanted it big—teased and popped. We fought about how I dressed. We fought about the appearances I made at clubs late at night. He had this idea that I was out partying all night and having fun. Well . . . I was, but I was getting paid. It was part of my job. I would have loved for him to come to the parties with me but he had to get up early to go to work the next morning. So when I was rolling in around three in the morning he was rolling over in bed getting ready to get up in a few hours.

I hated his friends, who were computer people, business executives and also listeners of my show. Anytime I came around I was Wendy from the radio and there would be a million questions about what was going on with Whitney Houston or some other star. I was like a novelty act. They were so corny.

At least Robert understood what I did for a living because he worked at a radio station, *my* radio station. His friends thought he married me for the glitz and the money. I could say a lot of bad shit about my ex-husband but I know he didn't marry me for the money. In the end he tried to sue me for the money but he didn't marry me for the money. And I didn't marry him thinking I would be able to "son" him because he made so much less than I. Women "son" a man by disrespecting him and taking his balls. I never wanted to do that. It's hard to take command if your woman has a bossy personality and makes so much more money than you. But men have to step up. I let Robert have his balls. Yes, I let him because he didn't have them to take for himself, which was another problem. I don't care how much money you make or don't make or what your career is, a man needs to step up and be a man in his household. We fought about that, too.

We mainly fought about my hours and rock 'n' roll lifestyle. There was a lot of jealousy from him. Robert was the low-level account executive getting a fraction of what I was making. I'm the popular deejay getting hundreds of dollars just from one of my appearances. I guess that hurt him. He's the account executive coming in at seven after working a full day and I'm the deejay coming in at three in the morning after a few Heinekens and some coke. He did not have a coke habit and did not know about how severe mine was.

The fighting was not physical but verbal, and it usually started after I came in from an appearance. It was mostly him saying, "I grind all day and all you do is sit behind a mike and party all night." That must have been the way it seemed to him. I'm making all of this money and this whole entertainment thing requires less education—you can be an eighth-grade dropout and still be successful in radio. It requires less physical time. I could sleep until noon because I was working the evening shift at KISS from six to ten. I was the star of the station. I was also a syndicated radio personality, so I was getting checks from all over the place. I was getting eighty thousand from KISS, but I was also getting paid boo coo bucks from a syndicator in Japan. The Japanese, who love hip-hop, wanted to have that radio presence from New York and I was "it" back then. There was also the side money from personal appearances.

My other half, though, is a guy on the grind with one of the lowest-paying jobs at the station. He didn't get the big accounts, the Pepsis and the McDonalds, he had to hustle and sell the mom and pop accounts—the local car dealerships and mattress companies—which was far more work, with far less pay. So looking back I understand his anger. The frustration just got to be too much. He just couldn't take it and the fights became more and more frequent.

The final fight? Who knows what it was about? But I do know that homeboy did something that I could never forgive. He spit in my face. I mean a big hocker that came from down low. And that was the last straw.

I did not react terribly. I didn't curse him out and try to scratch his eyes out. I calmly called my parents, though. It was one of those fights that had me calling my best friend, Lisa, to come to the apartment to lend me emotional support. He pushed her out of the apartment into the hallway. He eventually left our apartment though and went back to his parents' house. Neither one of us was a cop caller and at that point I was very popular on the radio. We both knew that calling the cops would be like a big blowup. And the last thing I wanted was publicity about my personal life. Bad enough that people in the building knew who I was. The picture my husband and I portrayed was as a successful deejay and her equally successful husband, except he always represented something that he truly wasn't.

That had a lot to do with why the marriage ended. Misrepresenting yourself when you're in the entertainment business can become an especially frustrating proposition. You can't keep up the act forever.

I was everything that I represented then and have been more so if I hadn't had to pay for two. I didn't mind that, though. And I repeat for the girls reading this book: Don't let finances deter you from love. But you have to see the forest for the trees. You have to understand that there is going to be a certain amount of frustration on your man's part if he doesn't have money. Not making as much as his woman can wear on the psyche of a man. And it certainly wore down my first husband's psyche because I knew he must have lost his mind to go so far as to spit in my face.

I think I spent the whole night talking to my family and Lisa. He spent the whole night on the phone with his family and *mine*. But I had already made up my mind. I was leaving him. I knew that this was a definite decision because I saw that having children with him would only make things worse. I had seen his W2s—if that's what you can call them when they're that low—and knew that if we continued, our financial burdens would fall on me. I was making a lot of money for that time but I had no indication that I would survive in the game and ultimately do as well as I'm doing right now. What I was looking at was that this money was fine for me and I could handle marrying down financially, but what would happen when we added a kid or two to the mix? We had no property, I was driving a little Eagle Talon, and he was driving a beat-down Volvo, the same car he was driving when I met him. I said to myself, "You have to correct this picture before it gets out of hand."

And correcting the situation for me was not going to a marriage counselor. I wanted it to end. The man had spit in my face. I felt like the next expression of frustration was going to be hands-on physical abuse. That's what I saw coming. And, thank God, I got out before it came to that. My girlfriend had witnessed the fight but I don't remember if she actually said to me, "Wendy, just leave." I do remember her being very supportive. My sister suggested counseling. But she is happily married to her college sweetheart. She's also very conservative. See a marriage counselor? Well, I felt like when it's over, it's over. Some things just cannot be fixed. And when my sister suggested it, it made me mad. I felt like I was not getting the kind of support from her that I needed. I called up my parents and told them what happened and they said, "Wendy, we are behind you for whatever." I needed to know that because I was feeling like if you weren't with me, you were against me.

At first I believed I was married for the long haul, for better and worse and all of that. That's the way we were raised. My parents have been married for more than forty-five years. I have never seen my father sleep on the couch or have to get a hotel room because he and my mother could not get along. I have never heard either one of them call the other out of their name and that "modern-day" stuff that "modern-day" couples do. Somehow, despite my parents' perfect marriage, I knew that this was not reality for all. My parents didn't teach me that it wasn't real, I just somehow knew. It must have been my futuristic vision. I always believed that divorce was an option for a reason. But five months? No, I expected the marriage to last longer than that.

My next step after I decided this was over was to figure out the details. How was this divorce thing going down? I knew I needed an attorney, so I opened my trusty Yellow Pages and found a lawyer. He was a white guy and I met him at his office and told him what I wanted to do. He hipped me to a few things I did not know. Even though our apartment was in my name, I couldn't just kick my husband out. If I left with him there, I could be accused of abandonment and he could stay there. And if he didn't pay rent—which he couldn't afford alone—guess whose credit would get further fucked up?

Thanks to my futuristic vision, I came up with a plan. I had a talk with myself and mapped it all out. I had no reference points, nobody to talk with, nobody to call. My parents were with me but that was only emotional support. I couldn't go to them for "what to do." They had never been through anything like this. My friend Lisa was great support but this was my mess. Besides, I've always been a good plan hatcher.

My first step was to get him out of the apartment. The following morning after he left for work, I met with the property management at my apartment complex and told them what was going on and that I was moving. I knew they would hassle me about breaking the lease in the middle of the term but I told them, "I'm having a domestic violence problem and if anything happens to me, I'm naming you in a lawsuit. You have enough apartments in here you must make one of them available for me. I only need a one bedroom." They immediately found me an apartment. This was really a no-lose situation; after all, I was still renting from them.

The next thing I had to do was figure out how to get rid of *his* stuff because I knew he wasn't going to leave. When I first approached him about leaving he said, "Well, you can move out if you want. I'm not leaving. But I do want a divorce." And I told him, "Fuck you, muthafucka, I want a divorce, too."

I don't blame him for not wanting to leave. Hell, this was a really nice apartment with a Manhattan view and everything. It was the best he ever lived. But the problem was we were paying about thirteen hundred dollars a month and the apartment was in my name. He couldn't afford it by himself. And I was just getting my credit together. I did not want to leave him with anything to ruin my name.

After meeting with property management, I called a professional moving company, one of those big ones. I knew not to pack his stuff myself and if anything was broken or missing he could say I did it. I got some professionals who were insured. They would be responsible for everything and vouch that I didn't touch his stuff. I told them that I was going through a messy divorce and that I needed his stuff moved without any problems and I needed them to keep good records or I would sue.

The next morning he left for work around seven o'clock. Father & Son movers were waiting around the corner for me to call as instructed. I had Skeletor and Lisa sitting around the corner behind the movers. I needed all eyes on the movers as I packed my own stuff. When he left at seven o'clock, the movers were there in minutes and me and Lisa were like Lucy and Ethel packing up my shit while four workers were packing up his. I had already arranged for his stuff to go to a storage place. I gave him everything we collected as a couple, including the gifts that people gave us for the wedding, and I instructed the movers to put it all in the storage room I had reserved for him. I'm glad I had the movers to verify everything because that motherfucker actually accused me of stealing his Sony Trinitron in the divorce papers.

I made sure I had a stack of money, because you know that movers want cash. And they got paid handsomely. I was a nervous wreck the whole time, smoking cigarette after cigarette. The apartment looked totally lived in prior to him leaving in the morning but by the time he got home at six in the evening there was a note that I left with the doorman (who only knew us as Wendy from the radio and her husband—a happily married couple) and a key to his storage room.

I made sure to put the note inside of a sealed envelope because I didn't want to be accused of embarrassing him. The note basically read, "Fuck you, I have moved. You have thirty days to get your shit out of storage." I paid for one month in the storage unit because I didn't want to be countersued for something fucked up.

I thought of everything. Lisa had never been through this, so while they were there for me and very supportive, they couldn't offer much advice. But I had my futuristic vision.

I know when he got that note he was totally pissed. He didn't know what to do and didn't know where I went. I guess he thought this young, dumb girl would be running back to Mommy and Daddy. He kept sending notes to my parents' house via his Manhattan attorney. The notes would get sent back with a note that read: "She does not live here."

I checked into the Marriott in Times Square, right down the street from KISS. My apartment was ready but I was scared to go there. Scared of what? I don't know. It was a fear that I can't explain. I guess I was scared of the repercussions. I did what I had to do, but I knew that there would be consequences, things I would have to deal with on my own.

I didn't invite Skel and Lisa to the hotel to sit around, slapping high-fives and laughing about moving him out. Yeah, I played you, muthafucka, but what are you going to do, follow me? If he did decide to follow me home, he would have been following right to the Marriott. I stayed there for a week, ordered great meals from room service and had plenty of time to think.

I did eventually move into my apartment, which was ready when I moved him out. And he eventually found out where I lived by having me followed. That was easy because we still worked together.

The Monday after the big move, I went to work and told Vinny and Charles Warfield, his boss, exactly what I did. They made sure he stayed away from my side of the building and there was a lock inside of the studio. He never physically approached me at work.

But the workplace had become increasingly difficult for me. Robert started talking shit about me at the station. I was even pulled aside by one of the bosses and asked if I could continue to work with him, because if I couldn't they would let him go. He had whispered to coworkers things like he had tricked me and bought me a cubic zirconia for an engagement ring. He and I both knew the truth—that I picked out the damned cz myself! I knew he couldn't afford a real diamond and, no, I was not walking around with a fifth of a karat on my finger.

But even with the badmouthing, I didn't want him fired. I knew what he was making and I was not trying to strip anybody of their livelihood. All I wanted was a smooth transition. At that point I hadn't been served with divorce papers. And my divorce attorney was just getting everything together to serve him. The one who served first, my attorney told me, would have the advantage.

One day I walked into work and there was a white guy waiting for me at the front desk. That wasn't unusual because there was always somebody there trying to give the jocks free stuff and this guy had a couple of sneaker boxes in a Model's bag. I thought it was free sneakers.

"Hi, Wendy?"

"Yeah," I said.

"I'm Pete from Model's," and he hands me the bag with the sneaker boxes. And he left. When I opened the boxes, they were filled with bricks and divorce papers. It was so slick all I could say was, "Oooooooh. You got that off!" I had just gone to the bathroom to take care of my habit and was all excited about opening these gift boxes, and "Pow!" I get hit with divorce papers. Pret-ty clever.

In his papers, in addition to accusing me of stealing his Sony Trinitron, he also was looking for alimony money to be able to "maintain the lifestyle to which I am accustomed." He was asking to be taken care of, a man who was eleven years older than me.

The reason for divorce was "irreconcilable differences." My countersuit was fair. I didn't ask for a thing. The only thing I wanted was an annulment to say this thing never happened. But in New Jersey you could not be granted an annulment if the marriage was consummated.

I just wanted to get it over with as simply and quickly as possible. But this fool was trying to push to have the divorce hearing in New York where he stood a better chance of getting money. This was a five-month marriage with no kids and no property. He was eleven years my senior and spit in my face and all I was thinking was, "Let it go, man! Why are you fighting?!"

This five-month marriage took about a year and a half to dissolve. What finally happened was that he ran out of money. He couldn't pay his New York attorney. I found out because during a meeting between my attorney and his attorney, his told mine that he was not handling the case anymore because my husband had not paid him. And while he didn't get any money, my attorney certainly got his, being hit off for a year and a half for a divorce that should have been an open and shut case.

But I didn't mind spending a dime because in addition to getting legal advice from the attorney he also gave me plenty of life lessons and financial advice.

He told me, "You know, Wendy, you really ought to look at investing all of this money you're making." And he connected me with a buddy of his at a major investment company. I actually looked forward to meeting with my attorney because we would spend most of the time just talking. We seemed to talk about everything *but* my simpleton husband.

So after his attorney stopped representing him we were able to get a court date in New Jersey. I showed up with my attorney and my sister, who was still being very conservative but I pulled her along anyway. I had the attitude that I was ready for the rest of my life. But I was still scared. The divorce happened the way it should have a year and a half too late—I signed the papers and it was over. He never showed up.

So for people who think you need two signatures on divorce papers to get divorced, you don't. People who think they don't happen because a party is unwilling, I'm here to tell you that they do happen. People who think they need this whole corral of friends and family. No you don't. You can go by yourself. And always, even if you live a rock 'n' roll lifestyle, make sure you have at least one conservative outfit—a business suit or conservative dress—in your wardrobe.

This dummy had the nerve to mention my "rock 'n' roll" lifestyle in his divorce papers. He said I was coming in consistently at three in the morning. But anybody who took time to know what I did for a living would understand why. But why didn't he point to the real deal? *(Whisper: My cocaine addiction.)* I guess he knew, like I did, that my habit was not the reason for our problems. In fact, my habit didn't seem to bother him much at all.

In court, I represented the opposite of what he said I was. I had on my conservative outfit and conservative hair. I had the look of a sensible woman, just in case he decided to kick in the door and represent himself at the last minute. And trust me, brother man knew how to lay it down if he had to. People actually bought his bullshit. (Hell, I did.) He would have had me looking like this wild, rock 'n' roll chick who drank and hung out till all hours of the night. Fortunately, he never came. And the divorce was done (finally) lickety-split. I even made sure that I got rid of his name. I didn't want to be Mrs. So-and-So ever again. I still have the divorce documents. They give me chuckles.

So my five-month marriage was over. He didn't get a dime. And, well, I did get something out of it. The ring. I never gave it back. I wanted to keep it. I still have it. It serves as a joke and a reminder of how real I always kept it with myself and others.

CHAPTER 8

Beauty and a Thug

She's so beautiful. He's a thug.
They're so perfect. They're in love.
—JAHEIM

I MET KEVIN back in the spring of 1994 at Skate 22 in Union, New Jersey. He was there with Mr. Cee, a local deejay who was spinning at the rink, which doubled back then as a happening nightspot. Big Daddy Kane was performing that night. And I was there on an appearance for HOT-97. Kevin was there with a bunch of his Brooklyn dudes promoting some party or something. I didn't really notice him at first.

I was surrounded by my entourage—Skeletor and my security, Bulge, and a few other guys—and while they would never try and block my flirting, they did provide me with a certain amount of insulation from the world. But I was approached by one of Kevin's boys (who is still in our cipher). He said, "You are always talking about roughnecks on the radio. You see that guy over there. That's the man you've been describing."

At the time, MC Lyte's "Roughneck" song was very popular

and every time I played it I would chime in about wanting a roughneck for myself. Kevin's boy apparently was an avid listener and knew this.

"Yeah, he wants to know when you two can hook up and get your Pathfinders dirty together," said Kevin's boy.

I thought that was so hot because you know guys are so into keeping there cars clean. I was impressed. And he was looking every bit the part. So I took the number. But it was no biggie because I had taken numbers before. I was just never big on callbacks and dating. I was so protective of my cipher and so protective of the shit I was into that I didn't really want anyone outside of it too close to me. I didn't want anyone to know the truth—that I was really a scared little girl from the suburbs with an ugly secret.

The way Kevin approached me was intriguing, though. It was bold without being in my face and I liked that. I later found out he did it that way because he did not want to be publicly turned down by "the big mouth bitch from the radio," as he knew me. He had heard me talk about wanting a thug and I guess he was testing the waters to see if I was really looking for a real roughneck or just talking shit. But just in case I didn't want one, he didn't want to play himself either. I thought that was a nice way to go about it.

I collected my evening's pay and left the skating rink to get to my next date—with the white lady. I smiled and waved good-bye to Kevin with my fingers. But I don't think then I had any intentions of calling him.

The next day I was at the station and about to take a break. I was cleaning out my bag in the studio between songs, looking for something to use for a quill. I had just gotten a package delivered from my Bronx dealer in my usual McDonald's bag with the fries on the top. I found a piece of matchbook at the bottom of my pocketbook, which was always my favorite kind of quill because a straw was so dirty to me. I was always careful about what I used as quill. I always factored in someone going through the garbage. If you go through someone's garbage and you see a straw cut at a particular angle, you immediately know what's up. If you saw a matchbook bent, it could have been from someone picking their teeth. And I was always careful to rinse off my matchbooks before throwing them away because there would be residue. Above and beyond everything, paranoia had definitely set in and was very much a part of my getting-high experience at that point. I had deep paranoia about everything, which comes with a three-gram-a-day cocaine habit.

Kevin's name and number were written on that piece of matchbook. As I was holding it and preparing to take my break, I paused. I don't know why. There certainly wasn't anything different about Kevin because I had not even spoken to him.

It was three-thirty in the afternoon. I recall clearly because it was right before the four-play at four. The four-play at HOT-97 was a very busy time back then as opposed to right now—which is busy from the moment I hit the floor running at two o'clock. But back then only the four-play at four was really busy. So I usually took a little time for myself just before. Instead of going to the bathroom to start on my package I said to myself, "Let me call this guy back. What the hell." I knew once I used this matchbook cover for my habit, his number would be lost forever.

On April 8, 1994, I paged Kevin. He called right back. And the first thing I noticed was his sexy, raspy voice. I told him who I was and said, "Look, I get off at six o'clock, you can meet me downstairs after my shift. If not, fine. We don't need a formal date for you to impress me. You don't need to go out and buy me flowers or anything. I certainly am not going to trick myself out for you, either." He laughed. I liked that.

That was just typical Wendy—even to this day, even sober. I don't have a lot of time to waste with people. And as far as telling him that I wasn't going to trick myself out for him, that, too, was typical Wendy. I just wanted him to be prepared. What was I dolling up for? I bare my soul on the radio. And besides, I looked as cute as I ever did the night he met me (which isn't as cute as I doll myself up today, by the way). Back then, I was never one to want to draw attention to myself.

Hell, I was already five-feet-eleven inches—that was attention enough. Wearing heels and all of that was definitely not part of my program. And it certainly would not have been a part of an outfit for a date. I've ultimately always felt that people should accept me as I am. And if they didn't, well I had a package waiting for me at home. Hell, it might be in the bathroom in the middle of a date, which I really wasn't too interested in doing back then anyway. Being in a world of my own paranoia, I didn't want people coming up to me and saying, "Hi, Wendy!"

I might be sweating or my jaw might be winding. Or my eyes

may be so glassy and big that I couldn't focus. I didn't need that kind of attention. I didn't need anyone peeping my little secret.

But I called this Kevin guy anyway. And before he could tell me whether he was coming to meet me or not, I cut him off and told him, "I'm about to go into a stop set; either you'll meet me in front of my job at six or you won't. Bye."

When my shift was over, I came outside and there he was standing outside his tricked-out green Nissan Pathfinder. Mine was black and done up like a dude's truck with black tinted windows. It was parked down the block.

I thought a lot about my safety after my divorce, so I got a car that would conceal me well, one that no one would think I'd be driving because it was very masculine looking. And I made sure to be as low-key as possible because I never really had a man to hold me down.

Not even my ex-husband, who was a big-body man, but was corny to the new ways of the hip-hop streets. I've had a few boyfriends before him who were financially secure and could provide that, but none with the complete package. There was a doctor who had a couple of Porches and a big house, and there was an aerospace engineer. They were real relationships where they would come home with me for Thanksgiving. And I never cheated on any man. That has never been my thing. It was always one man at a time.

Those types of men, I found, really were not my type. But that seemed to be all I was dating. Even when I was in college I had two serious boyfriends—one lived in Montclair, New Jersey, and came from a nice, prestigious family and the other graduated from Boston University and was eleven years older than I was. He was a frat man.

But who did I really want to date in college—the boys who lived in the projects behind my school. That's who I hung out with, smoked weed with, had the best time with. Who was I really attracted to? The thugs. The thugs always made me feel protected and gave me respect. They always had fun and excitement with them. But I could never bring them home to my parents.

Once I divorced Mr. X and had weathered the storm and basically told my family, "Look, fuck you, I'm getting a divorce and moving on!" I bought my condo in Florida, right on the beach. I renovated it, raised the ceiling and domed it out. I bought all new furniture for it. And I never rented it out. That scored major points with the parents who saw that I could handle my business. They thought, "You know through all of that she survived. And we didn't lend her anything but emotional support."

After going through that I was willing to come out of the closet with everything—well, almost everything. I was certainly willing to let the world know of my love for the thugs. And here was one waiting for me at the end of my show, right on time. And even though I told him not to do anything special, I noticed that he had on new clothes—a green Pelle Pelle outfit. I remember thinking it was the wrong color for his skin tone, which was the same complexion as mine. People our complexion shouldn't wear that pea soup shade of green, it makes us look real sallow.

Aside from the color, his outfit fit him well. He looked good.

He flashed me that smile that kind of cut through all that Brownsville thug action. It was the same smile that I noticed at the skating rink—pearly whites, no gold caps, just bright. Oh, and his voice. Damn!

I got in his Pathfinder and went to Brooklyn to close his shop. He owned a beauty parlor on Cortelyou Road. And on the drive over the Brooklyn Bridge I knew I had the potential to fall in love with him. His smile, his personality . . . you know how attractive a thug is when he lets down his guard. I mean he's still a thug, but there's something more there.

I got out all of my obligatory questions that would eliminate him from serious contention: "Do you have any kids?" and "Are you currently in a relationship?" and he answered them both correctly—"No."

He was twenty-three years old, younger than I was. And he wasn't clinked up with all that baby's mama drama. How rare is that in this day and age? It was hard to believe.

I went back to his apartment. It was a real mess, so much so that even after our dating became more serious I never spent the night there. It was a real bachelor's pad and there was no way no decent chick would spend any amount of time up in that piece. Yuck!

I wouldn't stay there even if I brought some shower shoes and a big-ass bottle of antiseptic. But you know what? It was *his* apartment. He wasn't living off his mama or some girl. And I loved that. He let me know that he had been on his own since he was a teenager. He had his own business, a car and his own place. He was a catch. His car was in his name. Yes, I checked. I looked in his glove compartment while he went into the store and found the registration. I had to do that because it seemed too good to be true. That's the only time I have ever sneaked . . . but it was with good reason. I was thinking that I could really fall for this guy and I don't need my feelings to be based on a lie. So if this car is registered to a woman, it better be his mother.

By the time we finished closing up his business and going to his apartment I felt safe enough to say I wanted to eat. And he asked me where I wanted to eat and since I'm not a date drainer I suggested Houlihans in Weehawken, New Jersey. The food was not expensive. I saw the guy's apartment. He was a hardworking man and I was not going to try and drain his pockets.

Hey, where we were headed, there was plenty of time for that. Better yet, I thought, he will fall so hard for me that eventually he will *want* to drain his pockets for me. And that's exactly what happened. And I'm not just talking about money. I'm talking about time and energy—the important things. But on this date, I ordered a salad (this is the one time I did not keep it real because what I really wanted was the ribs, mashed potatoes, a big dessert—the works). I was ready to tear down the house as far as food was concerned—especially after smoking that Brooklyn chocolate. But I had on a pair of tight Levi's and couldn't risk a blowout.

At the time I was the spokesperson for Mac Wear clothing. Not a lot of people had a clothing contract back then and I was getting a very healthy five figures to wear their clothes. Nowadays celebrities sport clothes for the exposure. I was wearing a Mac Wear shirt loose because I had no boobs back then and a loose belly. I had on a pair of tight jeans, though, and some Timberlands. I looked cute.

We sat and talked for a while and I was starting to ask myself, "Where does this date go? Do we go back to my house or what?" I drank Heineken's right out of the bottle with no glass because I was that type of chick. And I wasn't into the champagne yet. I wasn't an "industry" chick. I would go in, do my job, go home. I would make my appearances, collect my money, and go home. I didn't realize that the rest of the industry was drinking Cristal. See, I had this habit and my habit didn't allow me to be around other people. When my job was over I wanted to go home, close my apartment door, pull out my quill and continue my very own private party.

After we left Houlihans we went back to my place. I owned a condo in Florida, but was renting a beautiful prime duplex penthouse in Jersey City that cost me almost three-thousand dollars a month. It had two bedrooms, three bathrooms, a washer-dryer, a huge Jacuzzi tub, lots of marble and two balconies with unblocked views from the George Washington Bridge to the Brooklyn Bridge.

I could see Kevin's eyes when he walked in. He was shocked. I guess he thought the bitch from the radio made twenty-five thousand dollars a year like a schoolteacher. So needless to say he was impressed because he's a nigga and most niggas go out and buy a Benz right away. So with me driving a Pathfinder and being so damned cheap I guess he thought, "Oh, she's not really doing that well." But when he stepped into my place all of those thoughts went out of the window.

After he looked around, we settled in the living room. And we talked the entire night. We didn't have sex; we just talked, smoked weed and drank Heineken's out of the bottle. After that first talk he knew that my family was the most important thing to me and he could threaten me with telling them something. So while I was still doing drugs, I never mentioned it to him. That would remain a private matter between me and myself. And thank goodness he never asked or made any accusations because that would have been it. I would have had to tell him, "This relationship is officially over!"

Speaking of over, I was having a little fling with a security guard at the Gap. It was nothing serious. But I knew after my first date with Kevin that Mr. Gap had to go. I was never the kind of woman who was a player—who could have more than one man at a time. It was too much to juggle. And I certainly couldn't sleep with more than one man at a time and I knew after that first date that this thing with Kevin could certainly go there. So I called Mr. Gap and respectfully told him, "We're over." He had a couple of tee-shirts at my house and I packed them up and left them with the concierge at my building. It wasn't a funky breakup. And I didn't do him dirty because I believe if you do dirt, dirt comes back to you. I believe in karma. And I wasn't going to play Mr. Gap out like that by stringing him along.

I liked Kevin so much that I took him home to meet my parents. This was 1994 in the summer when my family—which consists of my parents, my sister, my brother and me—usually spend a lot of time together. This summer we were at my sister's house. She was there with her husband and my brother didn't have a serious girlfriend at this point. And here I come with Kevin. We had been dating for about four months and I was in love. It seemed as though everything was going well for me. My career was on point, so much so that my parents really couldn't say shit to me about Kevin. Inside I knew my family would eventually accept whoever I brought home as long as he loved me and made me happy.

At some point during the day, my mother got him alone and I happened to walk in just when my mother was asking him, "Why are your pants so baggy?" He wasn't offended; he handled it like a champ. I had warned him about my family and they lived up to the billing.

I didn't ask him to change or be on his "best behavior." I didn't tell him what to wear. I didn't ask him to put on any hard-sole shoes or pull up his pants. I figured if they were going to meet Kevin, they needed to meet Kevin, not some made-up man faking it to impress them. Believe me, I was ready for a battle if it came to that.

If anything, I tried to break him into my family, I didn't try and break them into him. And we ended up having a nice day. It turned out that my mother and I had a lot more in common than I knew. Before she met my father she was dating boys from very well-heeled New Jersey families. Her family was very excited about her getting clinked up with one of them. And then my father came along. They met on the beach. He was from Atlantic City. My mother's father (who I called "papa") protested up and down the street because my father was, you know, not the right class.

So coming there with Kevin, it was like they understood. They weren't as judgmental as I thought they would be. And most of all, I think from a father's perspective he might have been a little relieved. When I tell my father I'm going to the Terror Dome nightclub and I'm just leaving at eleven o'clock at night he calls me on my cell phone just to call and I guess he realizes the best time to catch me is at night and he knows I will probably be there until three o'clock the next morning and he asks, "Is Kevin with you?" and I tell him, "Yes," he feels okay about everything. In the end, he wants his little girl to be safe and he could see with Kevin that would not be an issue. Having Kevin with me, in my father's eyes is even better than having "security," which makes the situation sound so dangerous. Kevin was accepted as part of the family.

As we got more serious it became a task for me to keep my dates with the white lady *and* Kevin. It became tough to juggle. I had to strategize. Since that first night I saw Kevin every day. He would pick me up from work every day. I stopped smoking coke altogether. It was too sloppy. I only sniffed at work or wherever I could. But my habit had slowed down considerably.

By this time, he had basically moved in. There was no official announcement that we were living together and he still kept his apartment but I wanted him at my place. I liked waking up next to him and I damn sure wasn't spending the night at his place. He stayed with me. But it was very clear, very early that he would not be approving of me having a habit.

On one of our first nights he talked to me about the streets and seeing what things like crack had done to people he knew and he could not tolerate it. He talked about the death and destruction of friends and neighborhoods at the hands of coke and how too many people were locked up or killed behind it.

My break from my habit wasn't cold turkey. I slowly weaned myself off the stuff to the point where one day I woke up and just didn't have the desire to do it anymore. There was something else filling my void and I didn't have time, room or energy for the white lady. I just stopped. There was no rehab and thank God no major breakdown, no arrests, no full-blown busts at my job, no bad batches that put me in the emergency room. I just stopped.

And I didn't pick up another bad habit like drinking excessively but I continued to smoke weed. I had been smoking weed since the eighth grade but I never smoked weed after doing coke. When I did smoke weed I wanted my high to be pure so I didn't want to drink alcohol or anything. At the point that I stopped using cocaine I can say that I had a four-gram-a-day habit, four days a week. Now the heads will know what that is. Four grams is supposed to be shared among four people or at the very least by two.

And my sobriety opened the door to the next phase in our relationship: Engagement.

It was the summer of 1997 and I was hosting a party at a Manhattan nightclub, Mirage. Kevin was throwing the party and

SWV, Gina Thompson with Missy Elliott, performed. At some point during the night, Kevin had the deejay stop the party and called me to the stage. Kevin came onstage; there were some guys, dressed in tuxedo shirts, who dropped rose pedals at my feet. Kevin got down on one knee and asked me to marry him, right there in the middle of the club with everyone watching. And all I could think was, "Oh, my gosh!"

While the public "engagement" was romantic and nice (it even made the gossip section of the *New York Daily News*: "Radio star Wendy Williams to marry entrepreneur Kevin Hunter), I really wasn't feeling the ghetto engagement. Let's not sugarcoat it with an engagement. Don't get me a ring. Get me a necklace or something. I didn't want to wear something that symbolizes something that is not really intended. And I made that clear. And Kevin assured me he intended to make me his wife. He didn't believe in marriage, but he knew if he was going to get married, I was that woman. At this point, though, I was not feeling marriage. I was still recovering from my first fiasco of a marriage and I really wasn't looking forward to jumping back in that saddle.

But I sure loved having Kevin around. He brought so much to the table. As soon as he came onto the scene, I didn't need security. Kevin handled all of that stuff. He told me, "I don't know what kind of man you dated in the past, but I'm not having this. You're my woman and I'm holding it down."

I was delighted with that because at the end of the day, Wendy is still the little girl who wants to be taken care of, and not financially. (Start playing the pink music.) I want to be taken care of physically and emotionally. I imagine even Oprah wants to be taken care of. Because at the end of the day we are soft. And we are pink. And even if we wear a hard exterior, we want a hug. We want someone to tell us we are pretty no matter how much we make and we want a man to support us, not dog us. We want to be loved. We want to be in love.

I was falling in love.

CHAPTER 9

Hot in Here

I WAS AT A PHOTO SHOOT ONE DAY. The photographer was a lesbian. And I won't mention her name because I don't know whether or not she's out of the closet. Kevin and I were at this shoot for a party that he was throwing at the Roxy. While the photographer was getting her stuff prepared she handed me a magazine, *One Nut*. She flipped it open and asked me to read this one particular article. I started reading it and I said, "Hmm. This is *very* interesting. I'm bringing this to the radio."

The article talked about a gay rapper, which was something I had seen frequently in this business. But this article totally explained the ins and outs—so to speak—of the gay lifestyle and the whole controversy behind the gay rapper. So I brought it to the station and read it over the air.

I was working at HOT-97—I was back at the place where I started in New York. It was now a hip-hop station but was in the same place I had worked, 1372 Broadway, in the late '80s. It was the same place where my cocaine habit took full bloom.

On my first day back at HOT, I walked into the bathroom—not to get high, but to actually use the bathroom, and I'll be damned if that heating register wasn't still broken on the wall. I guess I hit it so hard with my big body that they couldn't fix it and just threw away the metal piece and never ordered another one.

It was a terrible, terrible, gruesome reminder of not only who I used to be but also who I still was. And all I thought was, "Oh my God, I can't wait to write my book and tell this story." It wasn't time then because I was still sniffin' and smokin'. But I was back now, with a vengeance. I was back at the top of my game. Emmis Broadcasting purchased KISS-FM. It already owned HOT, which was the same format. So when they purchased KISS they changed the format to the oldies and they brought me and DJ Red Alert from KISS to HOT, which was slowly taking over hip-hop.

I came back in the afternoon drive, which next to mornings is the most listened-to four hours on the radio. And in just a short period, my show was one of the highest rated in the city. I was already very controversial and very successful. But, boy, did this gay rapper thing set something off.

Do we know who the gay rapper is? I spoke to the writer and he just made up a story about a gay rapper. This story wasn't one man's story—it was a composite. You're not supposed to sit there and try to figure out who the gay rapper is but learn from the message of the story. But all people cared about was, "Who is the gay rapper?" That wasn't the question. Because going to industry parties I can point to two handfuls of gay rappers and another five fingers of lesbians. This is so commonplace in the business.

But I so loved sharing that story of the gay rapper with my public. That was phenomenal. One half of the folks were saying, "Great, great, great!" The other half were saying, "Shut up, you bitch!"

I was mostly getting the "Shut up, bitch!" from the artists themselves. Perhaps I was hitting a nerve. It seemed during this time, the mid 1990s, everybody was on edge, everybody was supersensitive.

The bling-bling era had started. People had taken off their leather medallions and the acts like the Jungle Brothers and De La Soul were fading quickly—replaced by something called "gangsta rap." People were rimming up their cars and buying expensive jewelry. And the stakes were getting high.

A few years prior, while I was still at KISS, the whole Puff Daddy, City College tragedy went down, where several people were crushed to death trying to get into a charity basketball event.

I was supposed to cover it. The day before Puffy and Heavy D had come up to the station to talk about the event. KISS was one of the sponsors of the game and gave it a lot of radio time. I was supposed to make an appearance, cheering on the sidelines.

I got off the air that Saturday at six and Skel and Bulge and I hopped in the car to go uptown. I had on my Reeboks and cheer-leader's skirt. I was ready. When we got to the block where City College is, the streets were crazy. Ambulances were everywhere and people were running wild.

When I got home that night, I learned that eight people were killed and twenty-nine injured when they shut the doors and refused to let people in. They had oversold the event and Puffy was in the middle of it all. *Oh, my God!* It was just one more thing to talk about and one more thing to be paranoid about in terms of the volatility of the streets and hip-hop, specifically.

I started making sure that when I was on appearances that I was perched next to a working exit door. I would never make my paranoia known. But Bulge and the guys knew the deal, what we were doing and why. We also made a habit of parking in the garage *not* closest to the club or venue. If something jumped off, everybody would be rushing to that parking lot. Few people would be going down the street where we were parked.

The culture of hip-hop had changed. People were sneaking guns into clubs, folks were getting shot on the street for stepping on new sneakers and stabbed in clubs for nothing. Fights were breaking out. It was a little scary. I had even been at a club where shots rang out on the other side of the club and there was a bum rush. Bulge got me a bulletproof vest to wear on my appearances. I was already paranoid from the cocaine and I wasn't taking any chances.

I even had a minor brush when a washed-up rapper (I don't even think she was ever big enough to even be washed up) named Boss sent a dead fish in a shoe box to me at the station as a warning. I had apparently said something about her on the air and she didn't like it.

Just as hip-hop was changing, I was changing the face of radio with my style. I wasn't talking soft and quiet storm-ish. I wasn't talking smooth. I wasn't talking happy-happy girl next door. I was gossiping and talking shit. It went from recapping what happened on *Dynasty* to recapping what happened in the clubs to talking about what was really going on with the stars of hip-hop.

My popularity was intense because the industry was changing. Artists were marking their territory. Lyrics were getting more and more violent. Rappers were going platinum—selling a million albums. Even in their heyday Big Daddy Kane and Rakim were struggling to go gold. A lot of the drug dealers of the '80s were now powerbrokers of '90s hip-hop. The shit was uglier and uglier and I was just steadily yapping. Every day I was in the middle of a battle—whether it was me and Lil' Kim, me and Treach, me and Mary J Blige, me and Sally Richardson. Or me and Puffy. Actresses, actors, rappers, singers, no one was exempt from my yapping. And the listeners loved to hate me. They were listening. And that was fueling it and made me keep going even more.

The day of the hootchies had arrived. Now hootchies and groupies have been a part of entertainment since the dawn of time. But now when a hootchie got dumped or was done wrong, she had a forum, a place to speak out—my show. She could pick up the phone and tell all. Sometimes, I would even put her on the air.

It was getting really heated. I started noticing different artists giving me the screw face if I was backstage at a station concert or out at an event. People were taking things very personally. Too personally. Around the time that things were heating up for me in the streets, Kevin came into my life. That was a blessing.

With him by my side, I didn't really care about the backlash I was getting. When you have a team—even when the world is against you—you feel like there is nothing you can't do. Above and beyond everything, Kevin made me fearless. I had boyfriends in the past who cared for me very much. Hell, my parents make me feel loved and comforted. But at the end of the day who's that nigga who's going to be there for me when I need a nigga, not a fucking hug? Kevin was that nigga. He made me feel that there was nothing that I couldn't accomplish. He made me feel that if anybody wanted to front on me with money at a club, he had my back. If anybody wanted to front on me at my job, he had my back. Not necessarily through thug means.

He would say, "Baby, I got you. Rest on a nigga. Trust me." And I did. It was nice to hear and know that I could.

I never wanted to test it. But there came a point where I had to. The gay rapper shit came to a head, as did some other things behind the scenes.

During a HOT-97 Summer Jam Concert, I was onstage hosting and getting booed to high heaven. I found it amusing. To me all those boos represented listeners. So I kept on talking. But backstage one of my bosses decided he would lower the curtain— right onto my head. The curtain was heavy velvet with a thick, metal rod along the base. The boos were replaced by laughter. I didn't care about the booing. But the curtain being dropped on my head by a boss was something else altogether. It was clear that I had no support at all from the powers that be at my station. I clearly saw that the second my numbers dropped, they would drop me. I clearly saw that I was not the darling of HOT-97, even if I was bringing in the revenue. So when it started getting heated with the boos, this boss, who was backstage, lowered the curtain. It hurt very much both physically and emotionally because I believe this bastard did it on purpose even though he apologized and said it was an accident. And I knew it was the beginning of the end.

I started noticing that people around the HOT offices didn't quite know how to approach me. I've met people since then who still work there who told me some of the talk that was going on. One guy, who gave tours around the HOT station, told me he came by the booth while I was on the air and told the tour, "Oh, that's Wendy Williams." And one of my coworkers who was nearby said, "Yeah, you know she's a bitch. Just leave her alone. Don't even think about opening the door."

A bitch? I had never done anything to this coworker that was even remotely bitchy, nor had I been a bitch in front of him. But when I heard it, I kind of liked that. Even if the image was getting me in trouble at my station. I was on a roll. I had a Web site that featured pictures of some high-powered executives and a rapper in a compromising position. I was talking about the relationship, making implications, coming right out and dishing all the dirt. I was telling it all about everybody.

No one was exempt.

There was a piece printed in the gossip section of the *New York Daily News* about one of my coworkers' then-boyfriend. I read it over the air giving my usual "Uh-huhs" and "Oh child, pu-leases" and making implications about his sexuality.

The funny thing is there had never been any problems with this coworker before, at least not on my part. But apparently there had been a little something brewing that I had no idea about on her part. After I read the *Daily News* piece, adding my two cents, I hear all this screaming in the hallway. My coworker approached me, screaming, "You always talking . . ." and blah, blah, blah. My shift was going on. But I wasn't physically on. I have not run my own boards in years. Skeletor was running the boards so I was hanging in the hall. There was yelling and girlie shoving, but no fists, no blows, no blood.

This is probably *the* most asked question. People constantly want to know about the HOT-97 situation and the "fight." The best thing I can tell you about HOT-97 in a nutshell is that I have no enemies at that station and I haven't for a long time from the highest position to the lowest. I have no enemies over there—not even Angie Martinez. I don't believe Angie hates me and I don't hate her. Did we fight? No, we did not.

This is my first time actually talking about Angie because there is so much there that people can make out of it and so much of which is really nothing. Let the girl live. She is not bothering me and I'm not bothering her. If I saw her at a party I'm not sure that we would hug but I wish her well. And I actually liked her last album.

Angie and I never had a problem until the end. In fact, I never had problems with any females that I worked with. From my teachers, Yvonne Mobley, Carol Ford and Champagne to the people I was suppose to teach like Angie Martinez and Coco. But today, with the jealous bitches biting my style, it is a different story. I had to wait fifteen years in this business to find absolute bullshit dealing with women in my career.

But that wasn't the case with Angie. It was all a big misunderstanding. So, Angie, here is a shout out to you that I won't make on the radio because people would make more of it than it is. But I wish you much continued success.

Could we work together again? Sure. We each have our own space—as it always was. Business is business and a true professional moves on, learns something and keeps a little feather tucked under their cap as a reminder. You never dwell on the past, but you must learn from it. I'm a grow-ass woman. I learn my lessons and keep moving!

The so-called fight with Angie was the last straw for my bosses. Actually it was an opportunity for them. They had been getting pressure from powerful people in the music industry to shut me up.

The best way to sum it up is Sean Puffy Combs was a very powerful man back then. And while he was not necessarily more sensitive than anyone else I singled out for gossip, he was wealthier and more powerful. If you turned on HOT-97 during any given hour, six of the eight songs played would be songs either produced or performed by Puffy. From Biggie, to 112 to Total to Faith to Mase, to Junior Mafia and Lil' Kim. He owned radio. And he was hard to ignore. And I knew with each word I spoke, I was practically writing my own ticket out of town.

As long as I was producing the numbers, I did my job and kept on yapping. But the controversy coupled with the rich and power-ful applying even more pressure finally did the trick.

I was called into the bosses' offices and told I would be taken off the air if I did not change my style. Which was not happening. They were asking me to become something different. I wasn't try-ing to hear it or sit out like some first grader being punished. Instead I sued them. And I packed up my shit and moved to Philly.

Unfortunately, people, because of a lawsuit and terms of that agreement I cannot tell you all the sordid details. But please know if the gag order is ever lifted, I'm blabbing everything!

I won an unprecedented lawsuit that had to be so far researched by my attorney that the only comparison was a case with Warner Wolf, a sports anchor from WNBC-Channel 4. And with the victory I had to be quiet.

I was number one when I left New York. And some may say how could a station let their number one jock walk? When you're a radio station and you're being beaten by a competing station, you buy them off. When I was at KISS I was whipping HOT's ass. So they buy KISS and bring me over to HOT. They change KISS to oldies and that kills the competition. WBLS had fallen so far off the map at this point they weren't even in the running. During the mid to late '90s if your favorite music was hip-hop and R&B there was only one place to go—HOT-97. And because they had no competition, I guess they figured, "Why do we need to pay this bitch? We will win that time spot no matter who's sitting in it." They were basically right.

I never got fired. That was another big misconception that people still get twisted. When I was taken off the air I had a considerable amount of time left on my contract and they would call me in to do commercials. My commercial time was so short that I could literally double-park in front of the station, run up, do my commercials and get back before I got a ticket.

But when you're an on-air radio personality who isn't on air you might as well be dead. And I'm too smart of a bitch to take a paycheck and go to Bloomingdale's while somebody tries to kill my career. Initially I figured if they were willing to pay me big bucks to do commercials, I had no problem with that. I figured it would blow over and I would be back on the air in no time. But a week stretched into two and by the time it headed to three, I thought, "Wait a fucking minute! These muthafuckas are really trying to kill my career!"

Thank God for Kevin and my mentality. We are not whores for money. I could have been on television a long time ago if I were a whore for money. But I wasn't willing to compromise or change to fit into somebody else's box just for the money. I would have stayed in New York under some very precarious conditions, probably still at HOT-97. A lot of things would have been different for me if I were a whore for the money. And I don't mean physically a whore for the money but willing to compromise my integrity and who I am for a dollar.

Kevin told me, "Wendy, you're trying to build something that's bigger than this picture. And you don't want somebody digging into your past history and say, 'Hmm, she took x amount to do this, so all you got to do is come to her with the right amount.' That shit catches up to you. And then you have no integrity."

And all a guy's got at the end of the day is your word and your balls. That's all you got. And once you break your word and somebody breaks your balls, you've got nothing. So I basically told HOT-97 to fuck themselves. The first sign that you have told someone, "Fuck you, I mean business!" is to stop taking their money. I only took HOT's money and laid all the good commercials for about three weeks—a paycheck and a half. I told them, "You can stop the money now, muthafuckas. We are officially at war!"

When you tell people—particularly white people—that they can keep their money, I'd rather fucking concentrate on this lawsuit, I'm trying to get out of my contract because you muthafuckas think that we're all slaves to somebody, white people, people in general, almost lose their minds. They think that money is the be-all, end-all. Well, it's not. They had built into my contract a "non-compete," which prevented me from taking another job in New York City for a period of eight months. Eight months off the air could be death for a career like mine. I had only two choices—stay in New York and die or move on.

I took my word and my integrity and went to Philly. It started out as a one-week fill-in on the legendary morning show that had started to fail the radio station miserably. The same team had been together for fifteen years. I had no idea really what they did there. When you live in New York you don't give a fuck about what anybody else is doing. You're on top, why look anyplace else?

All those people want to be where you are. So I went down there with that mentality, "When this week is up, that's a rap!"

But that week turned into a full-time offer. I couldn't work in New York for eight months. Most radio stations negotiate these non-compete clauses for three months. But you know you're the shit when your non-compete is more than six months and you're really the shit if it's more than a year. My eight months was considered a big deal.

So rather than sit home and watch my career die, I took the job in Philly. Kevin said, "Fuck it! Let's break out a new territory. Fuck it, we'll go down there, we'll turn it out and it's not far from New York. We can do this." And I believed him.

I wasn't there but a hot minute before shit started happening. My first week on the job I found out that I had a miscarriage, unbeknownst to anybody. And in my third week my new boss pulled me into her office and said, "Wendy, I don't want you to be a dinosaur. You have to change your style." *Change? Dinosaur?!*

And I wasn't just getting it from her, the hate in Philly during my first few months was incredible. When I first got there they did this survey: Ninety percent of the listeners had heard of me due to the proximity to New York. But of that ninety percent, seventy percent hated me. The station was getting calls like, "Oh, my cousin lives in Hempstead and he said this big-mouth bitch is nothing but trouble!" And this was even before I was officially on the air.

But I watched those numbers turn in a matter of months and

my approval rating started to flip. You can say you proved yourself when you go to a whole new city and do the damn thing. And I proved myself. When I got there the morning show in Philly was number fifteen. By the time I left, we were number one sometimes, alternating with the *Howard Stern Show* for the top spot. Some books we were number three and Howard was number two. In other words, I was doing the damn thing.

And when we left, we left reluctantly because Philly became family. When we left, we left with a sea of love. It was good. And that made coming back to New York all the more sweet. I came back from a positive situation into a full-circle moment.

Going to Philly was the best thing that could have happened to me. I went to Philly under some questionable circumstances and I turned that city out. And when I came back, instead of the drama I left, I came back to open arms. People were hungry for the *Experience*. They missed Wendy Williams.

Bitches had an open line in New York for four years. They could have come and taken over the spot I once held and made it impossible for me to come back and reclaim my crown. Bitches already on the radio, bitches who wanted to be on the radio, rap bitches who failed in the music business and were now trying the radio thing. None of them made the kind of mark that would dethrone me. There have been many imitators. For four years the spot was open. Yes, that station was still number one during that time but they were the only game in town. It wasn't through quality and great personalities. It was because they had no competition.

When I came back, I had no idea what to expect. But me and my people, we missed each other. And we cried when I came back. I was getting calls from people who were seventeen when I left who were now in their twenties and missed me dearly. When I came back that was some true love. I have a relationship with each and every listener from eighteen to eighty-four.

I am a big sister. I am a peer. I am a mother along with other mothers now. I am a wife in the struggle of working women. I am a daughter. I am an ex-addict. I have so much in common with so many different people that it's overwhelming to me. Even after a year people were still saying, "Welcome back, Wendy."

Women and niggas had four years to shit or get off the pot and no one was able to fill these size elevens. There have been others who have left the city and come back to a lukewarm reception. You have the chicks who tried to imitate me and people are flipping on them and prodding me, expecting me to have that same immaturity that I had before I left and come after them. But we don't need to bash others in order to make our experience great. The old Wendy sure would have. Sure! But the new Wendy, well, I couldn't be all the way mature, now could I? How boring is that? So I slip into pettiness from time to time to keep the game interesting.

You know how some people stop smoking cigarettes and then become like the worst anti-cigarette people out there? I'm not like that. They would say to a smoker, "Oh, you could get cancer!" Well, I would say to them, "Muthafucka, let me live my life! I know what you went through." Even though I'm a recovering addict, I'm not going around wagging my finger at people who I see on the stuff. That's not my place. Like Mary J Blige. She was a head. And God bless her for quitting. But she's so saintly now. Where's the fun?

And with my personality, it's the same way. The new Wendy is more compassionate, more pink (background music, please), more soft, but every now and then she has to let a little of that old Wendy shine. Now take that, bitches!

CHAPTER 10

Getting Off the Shit

I'VE GOTTEN HIGH AT WORK and in clubs. I've gotten high on highways in my car. I have even gotten high in an airplane bathroom. When you're an addict, you don't care about anything but getting high. You have a one-track mind. I was so caught up that I smuggled coke in various nasty cavities of my body because I could not be anywhere without being able to get high, and I didn't want to depend on making a connection wherever I traveled.

I've been to Jerome Avenue in the Bronx at three in the morning to cop drugs on several occasions because my dealer was too busy to deliver. I've had to wait for him on a specific corner for hours sometimes—and I would wait because I needed to get my fix.

Drugs are an unpredictable business. You can't rely on a drug dealer to be where he says he's going to be on time. You can't even rely on a drug dealer to charge you what he says he's going to charge. If he feels like doubling the price, you'll pay it because you want to get high.

Drug addicts are unreliable, too. You can't count on a drug addict to be a good mother, a good husband, or a good worker. You can't even count on a drug addict to look out for themselves. I put myself in some very dangerous and scary situations because I wanted to get high. There's no honor in the drug game, whether you're a user or a seller. I don't know what the fuck I was doing all of those years.

But I'm so glad that I'm out of it today. I'm so glad I left drugs and came back to life relatively unscathed. I don't understand how I managed to be a reliable employee when I was so deeply involved in the drugs, and the worst kind of drug at that— cocaine. Cocaine is the devil.

And I beat back that devil—with a whole lot of help. I didn't go to rehab nor did I involve a whole bunch of people in my recovery. I wouldn't have gotten off so quickly if I had involved a bunch of people in my quitting. The babying and hand-holding would have been a stumbling block and given me an easy out. I didn't have any easy outs.

I was given a unique opportunity to start over in my personal life. I had a chance to be happy, to be in love, to be a wife, to be a mother—to be everything that I saw for myself as a little girl in Wayside, rocking back and forth, plotting my future. This was it. I chose life.

When I met Kevin, I was heavily sniffing and smoking cocaine. But after our first date everything seemed to change. I don't even think to this day that he realizes how much he's changed my life. My family doesn't even realize it. You see, the picture would be that the guy in the suit would change all that. Not the thug.

But you know what it was? I met Kevin and realized I was falling for him and that he had a big mouth. People find out shortly after getting to know me how important my parents and their opinion are to me. So him threatening to tell my parents would have been a big thing. And Kevin's the type of guy who would have had no problem telling my folks.

But being around Kevin also made me not want to be around cocaine. He filled in whatever blanks coke was filling. After my divorce I realized I needed someone to roll with me; I didn't need to deal with another bullshit muthafucka who had to grind all day for a week to make what I make in two hours at an appearance. Kevin was in the grind with me. He had his own businesses, he threw parties for a living. He knew about the club scenes and that my appearances were not about fucking, picking up niggas and getting numbers. He knew that four-in-the-morning arrivals home and even being drunk in the back of a limo was not about being sexually promiscuous. He knew quickly that I was making it hot on the radio and, yes, a large part of me is that sharp-tongue chick that you hear. But he was beginning to know that was only part of my hustle. He was finding that I knew how to turn that off and be warm and pink. Sidebar: And if more high-powered women knew that, perhaps more high-powered women would have men.

You see these women with the big fucking mouths in the boardrooms and at work bringing that home and start saying dumb shit to their man like, "I make the fucking money and this is my fucking house, nigga!" See, that kind of bullshit might get you tough-girl points but you're never going to settle down with a real man. If you settle down, you're going to be stuck with a man who you will quickly get bored with—like the string of boyfriends that I had in the past who I was able to run over. I would say all kinds of shit to them and get away with it like, "What are you looking in my eyes for?" knowing I was all fucked up. "I was out last night grinding until four in the morning to make money and you're just jealous." In the meantime I might have just come out of the bathroom, and by the way, do I have anything under my nose? I would make sure that the man I dated never indulged so that (a) they wouldn't see the signs, and (b) if one of us was going to have a habit it was going to be me because I had the money to support it and I was getting it cheap. I really had the money for this and to pay my bills and buy whatever I wanted.

Kevin made me change my cell phone. "You can't be queen of the radio with this outdated thing," he said even though I hardly ever used it. He was the type of person who I felt comfortable with from day one. And once he was in, I wanted to make sure that what he saw and what I was, was as pure as he was. I'm not saying that Kevin was an angel. But he was real and honest with me. He was raw.

Kevin sideswiped me. He saved me from doing coke the very first day we met. For that one night, he took my attention away from something that was a near obsession for me for a very long time. I was getting down at least four or five days a week. The other days I was recuperating. The other days were probably because I had business to attend to, which involved looking people in the face and my on-cocaine behavior would not have been palatable.

My friends, who never knew about my habit because I kept it a secret, could not have stopped me if they knew. To them I was Wendy from the radio—their star friend. They couldn't care less that I was a cokehead. And if any of them had mentioned it and tried to say something to me, I probably would have cut them off. And they probably knew that, too. So I don't blame them for not saying something. Coworkers would rather talk about me behind my back than to see me recover from my addiction. I know they were talking because I could be in the green room waiting to do my shift, wildly high, sweating like it was 110 degrees, pretending to read a magazine but really using it to fan myself, and one by one coworkers would come in—one sending in the next—to see the spectacle. They wanted to observe Wendy sweating, fanning herself and, oh, wait a minute, isn't that a big brick under her nose? Funny thing is that I work with many of the same people today. But you know what? I cured myself; I solved my problems—and now I walk through there with a big smirk. No, I don't blame them for talking about me behind my back. Hell, if it was somebody else, I might have been talking, too.

That was who and what I was then. And I know now that I wasn't hiding anything from Kevin. He knew. He never caught me in the act. But my behavior was different when I was high. Cocaine is not the sleeping drug. He would be sleeping, it's three o'clock in the morning and I'm up. Not just up but wired, wide awake. I'd be on the couch at three o'clock, wide awake. Four o'clock in the morning, still awake. Five o'clock and I'd still be sitting up with my jeans and panties on, paranoid about something and too lazy to take off my jeans and panties.

The all-night binges or all-weekend binges stopped with Kevin around. I couldn't get high as often or as much as I had before spending my time with him. I had to resort to trying to sneak and use it around his schedule. When he would leave, I would sit down to no less than two grams at a pop. Because I would have to finish the entire package by the time he arrived, I could easily do three or four grams by myself in one sitting. I found the love of my life and I didn't want him to ever see that side of me. I even stopped cooking coke and returned to strictly snorting because how would I explain the bent-up, burnt spoons and the smell to my man?

Before Kevin, I cooked more than I sniffed. Cooking coke seemed to me to be a much cleaner high. But I liked it all. It's like when you sit down to a meal you have steak and potatoes. Now you can have that steak rare, well done or medium. You can have that potato baked, mashed, scalloped (you get the picture). It was the same way with coke for me. I liked it a variety of ways—cooked, sniffed, in a cigarette or a blunt—the latter two seemed like a waste to me. I liked my high too much to waste it in a cigarette or blunt. The one thing I never did with it was shoot it up.

I kept my cocaine in a plastic green container on my kitchen counter before Kevin. But I had to resort to hiding it when he moved in. I would keep a package in my bathrobe. In hindsight, I guess I was begging to be discovered. I mean all he had to do was put his hands in my pocket and there it was.

He never cornered me. He never busted me out. Even when I was acting strange from being high, Kevin never screamed at me or lectured me. He did something, the only thing, actually, that could get me to stop—he killed me with kindness.

Had Kevin confronted me, I would have had a comeback. Had he lectured me, I would have turned a deaf ear. But to kill me with kindness, well, there was no defense for that. There are a few artists who have killed me with kindness after I've said something about them on the air and believe it or not, they get a free pass from me. I tend to not talk about the ones who have killed me with kindness. Now if there is a really juicy story, everyone is fair game. But there are some who simply get a free pass.

People hear me on the radio and they assume if they come at me and if they threaten me and call me a bitch or worse that I will stop. But that only makes me come harder. I love that. I love the confrontation. (Note: Rappers don't read, so nobody tell them what I'm saying, okay? Because I still want to have something to talk about.)

Somehow Kevin knew this about me. I'd be in the middle of being fucked up. He would say, "What's the matter with you, yo!" He would get disgusted with me sitting there all night in the same clothes and still be there at seven in the morning. But he would leave it at that. He wasn't being confrontational, which was so out of character for him. I mean this was a man who was confrontational by nature. He's not the type to shut up about shit. Kevin has a nasty temper and yells and screams when he's angry and frustrated. We've had fights about other things. But about this, he was silent. I spent a lot of my sober time thinking about this and being upset with myself for betraying him.

I've known Kevin almost ten years, and my drug abuse was the only issue between us that he has let ride. Thinking back, that's how I knew he loved me as much as I loved him, from the jump. He didn't know what to do. He was at a loss. He wasn't trying to use me. He was stumped. So he kept quiet.

There came a point though when I stopped doing cocaine. I saw that it was really hurting him. We never discussed it but I was smart enough to know that my habit was hurting him. And it became too much work to try to pretend to keep the addiction from him. I certainly wasn't willing to say out loud that I was an addict. He didn't deserve that kind of woman. So, I stopped being one.

Once I met Kevin my priorities changed. The energy I put into getting high was now put into being with him and making this thing we were becoming grow. I didn't stop cold turkey. I didn't go through rehab. I didn't find Jesus. I just was weaned off the stuff the way a baby gets weaned off the tit.

At no particular point did I think about what I was doing to my body. Nor did I ever think about my own health and wellbeing. But now all of sudden I have this man in my life, who I want to give my best to and there was simply no room for "us" and the white lady.

And after the trial and all the other drama with HOT-97, there just didn't seem to be any more room for cocaine. When we moved to Philly, I left my habit and all the other shit right there in New York. I couldn't see trying to find a coke connection in Philly and I definitely wasn't traveling up and down the highway to New York.

They say once an addict, always an addict. I'll accept that title. I have no problem with that. If it wasn't for my addiction I would not be the fabulous woman I am today. I know, however, that inside I am not an addict. I am a wife. I am a mother. I am a daughter. I am a sister. I am a radio personality. I am Queen of New York. If you want to throw "addict" in there, too, go right ahead. Because I know there is nothing that could turn me into that person again.

Nothing. Ever!

CHAPTER 11

And Baby Makes . . .

I FOUND OUT I WAS PREGNANT THE WEEK I was hired to work in Philadelphia. I was very excited because by this time, I was very much certain that Kevin was the man I wanted to spend the rest of my life with. No, I wasn't looking to get married. And neither was he. But we knew we wanted to be with each other. I thought we would be doing our thing the way Goldie Hawn and Kurt Russell do their thing—commitment, kids and all that, just no marriage papers. Who needed that, anyway? I had been through that once and was not interested in doing it again. It wasn't necessary.

We were in a new town, fresh off the wretched stress of going through a trial and all of that drama back in New York. And now we were starting a new family. Things were turning around for us. The new station had put us up in a hotel until we found a place. I was anxious to find a home in the area and make a statement. I wanted people in Philly to know that I wanted to be a part of Philly. I already knew how they viewed New Yorkers—as people who think they're above it all and that their shit don't stink. I didn't want to appear to be a New Yorker who was using Philly as some springboard to get back to New York. I was fully prepared to spend the next thirty years in Philly. I planned on being like Mary Mason to Philly—someone really entrenched in the Philly scene. Mason is a very prominent, older woman who means a lot to politics, broadcasting and media in general. I was committed to Philly. So we found a three-bedroom apartment in the heart of Germantown—a three-bedroom because we were going to have a baby. The plan was to make sure we wanted to stay in Philly. Rent for a year, sell our place in Port Liberty, Jersey City, and buy a home in South Jersey.

Kevin was still commuting back and forth to Jersey City, where we had a condo in the Port Liberty Yacht Club. He was still taking care of his car detailing business, which I respected and he needed to do. We both spent weekends in Jersey City. But Philly was home.

We were still living in a hotel and hadn't moved into our apartment yet when I had my miscarriage. I had gone to the bathroom. There was blood in my underwear and on the tissue. And I knew it couldn't be my period. Kevin and I went to the hospital together and they said I'd lost the baby. Actually at seven weeks in my mind I didn't consider it a baby—it was seed. But it was painful all the same.

Perhaps it was the stress from the trial and the HOT-97 drama. Perhaps it was the pressure of the new city and having to reestablish myself in this new market. I don't know what caused it. The doctors said it was common for women to naturally abort early on—it was not unusual at all. But I was very paranoid. I wanted to make sure that everything inside was okay and that I took every precaution to make sure it didn't happen again. I didn't feel that the doctors in Philly gave me the best care. I felt like a welfare woman going to the hospital—no disrespect to those on welfare. But I'm not checking for bad health care. And to white doctors, we're all the same. I come in there with my man—no wedding ring. That sends one image. I had no insurance—my job was so new that I had to wait three months for the insurance to kick in. That sends another image. I'm crying and carrying on and here is my man, this thug. That sends yet another image.

And although there was a big to-do about my coming to Philly with newspaper articles and television coverage, I'm sure this doctor could care less about urban radio and he had no idea who I was. In fact, no one in the hospital knew who I was. I was treated like any other unwed mother with no insurance. I meant nothing to them. I got the "nigger treatment."

So I called my doctor in North Jersey and made an appointment for her to check me out. The following week after my show, I got on the Amtrak train. I didn't want to deal with driving. Kevin met me at the train station. We went to the doctor's together. I was strong. I did my crying on the train ride. I did most of my crying when he wasn't around because he didn't need a weak woman. I knew if he knew how heartbroken I was, he would drop everything and just be with me 24-7. He would sacrifice his business and everything. But that's not what I wanted. So I kept a lot of my emotions hidden from him. He met me, we went to the doctor and she gave me a D&C (dilation and curettage), where they vacuum you out and make sure you don't keep bleeding—and make sure your womb is free from anything that can give you an infection—and will be ready to receive another child, if that is God's will. My doctor basically gave me a clean bill of health. Kevin dropped me off at the train. I had to force him to return to his business and told them that I would be all right. I had this. I went back home. And I got up the next morning and did my show, like nothing had happened. I didn't miss a beat.

Less than two months later, I was pregnant again. What a blessing. Everything was going to be all right. My show in Philly was really taking off. Kevin's business was doing well. We were enjoying our living arrangement. And we were pregnant again. In the summer when I was in my third month, we started buying furniture for the nursery, which was the bedroom off the master suite. By August, I was in my fourth month and shopping for baby clothes. I was starting to show. I had stopped doing nightclub appearances at this point, but was still making some daytime appearances. And everywhere I went people were congratulating me. I shared this entire experience with my radio audience, as I share things with my audience today. They were part of my growing family.

One night in September 1998, Kevin and I were in the bedroom of our Philly apartment watching a movie about the Temptations. I had fallen asleep on the movie and woke up because the bed was wet. We had a king-size bed and there was a puddle on my side. I thought I had urinated on myself. So I got up and went to the bathroom. I came out with this curious look on my face and said to Kevin, "You're not going to believe this . . . but I think I peed on myself. I have to change the sheets." We both had a little chuckle over it. I changed the sheets and I got back in bed. We were both wide awake watching television and I felt more water and it wasn't coming from my bladder. I looked at Kevin and said, "My water broke! I'm about to have the baby."

By this time I had found a regular gynecologist/obstetrician in Philly. We called her and she met us at the hospital. It turned out that my water did break. They tried everything but I lost the baby. They couldn't save her. Yes, I know it was a "her." We had even picked out a name for her when we found out just weeks before that we were having a little girl. It's too painful to even utter her name now. But, yes, she had a name. She had ten little fingers and ten little toes. And she had a perfectly formed face. She was a baby. She was five months into gestation.

We didn't have a funeral because I felt that it would be too much for my fragile emotions to take.

All I wanted to do was get back to being strong. And I wanted my husband to continue on with his business. I didn't want to be a wet noodle because he had shown me he will drop everything for me. He was my pillar of strength during the trial. He was constantly lavishing me with gifts and surprises. He was holding it down for me at social gatherings and family events. He had shown me he was down for me. And I didn't want to have to put him through that. It's nice to have that kind of strength supporting you. I didn't want to abuse it. Ever. I considered losing that baby something I could handle. I kept saying to myself, "I will not be weak. I will not be weak." I will check out of the hospital and I will get back on the radio. I will get back to work and I will be strong for the community. I will be strong for the sisterhood. I will be strong for my man and I will be strong for my mom and dad, who would have left Florida, flown up here and stayed with me for as long as I needed them. But I didn't want to burden anybody.

Kevin sat me down and had a long talk with me. "Maybe God doesn't want us to do it like this," he said. "We are meant to lead our community and maybe we aren't representing the right thing. Maybe God wants us to do it the right way. Maybe we're all out of order. Let's get married and *then* work on having a baby."

Married?!

This was a big step. Kevin was never the marrying type. He said he had never seen a marriage that worked. And while I had, I had been down that road before and it wasn't good. I was scared to death to do it again.

But maybe Kevin had a point. Maybe we were out of order in God's eyes. And the more I thought about it, the more I *wanted* to get married. I wanted to have his last name. I wanted to be a Hunter, legally, and in the eyes of God. And I wanted to wear a ring, not the ring he gave me with so much pomp and circumstance a number of years before. I wanted to wear *the* ring.

I know a lot of women soil their ring finger with friendship rings and long-term boyfriend rings. And Kevin had given me a beautiful diamond ring as an engagement ring in front of thousands at a huge party he threw for my birthday. But I felt like the "engagement" ring he gave me at my birthday party was a lie because neither one of us then had any intentions of getting married. That ring did truthfully represent our love for each other and we felt that ring and our love would be enough. It wasn't.

I wanted him on my health insurance. I wanted the same name on our passports. And I wanted for white America, as well as black America, to know that we are a family . . . for real. I wanted my child to have married parents. No disrespect to anyone who is living with a boyfriend with several kids and all that. But that's not what Wendy from Wayside wanted. I wanted the real deal.

Neither one of us wanted a big wedding in a church and all of that. We didn't need any presents. My homes—the Jersey City condo, the condo in Florida and my apartment in Philly—were already well laid out. I had the finest crystal, china and all of that. I slept on no less than 400-thread-count sheets. I didn't need another damn toaster.

I didn't want to wear a white dress—not because of the purity issues but because white makes me look fat. And we didn't want to spend all of that money. We'd rather put the money toward something else—like another house. Our love was beyond that showy shit. I didn't need to stand before a church full of people to show Kevin that I loved him and vice versa. Besides, just the thought of a big wedding—vomit.

So two months after the miscarriage, I ordered our marriage

license. We set the date—November 30. It was a Friday and gave me a chance to go to the Jersey City condo, which I hadn't been to in a while, and spend a nice weekend there. We were going to be married at the Jersey City Court House.

So after my shift, I drove to Jersey City. I changed into a little miniskirt and a black turtleneck and my stiletto ankle boots. I went to the condo and Kevin picked me up and we went to the courthouse. We were married by the Justice of the Peace who happened to be the brother of Grace Jones, the singer and actor. Our witnesses were one of Kevin's buddies and Grace Jones's brother's secretary. After we got married he dropped me off and went on to close his shop.

And that was fine with me. We were married. I had my new ring—most guys would have traded in the old ring for a new ring, but Kevin took the old engagement ring and made it into a necklace that I wear 365 days a year (the only time I take it off is for medical procedures). I had my wedding ring and my husband. I was Wendy Hunter.

I thought, now in God's eyes we will be more blessed. In January we took a late honeymoon and went on a cruise and had a great time. But when I got back all of the emotions of the seven-week miscarriage and the five-month miscarriage came flooding back. And while I continued to work and put on a nice face, inside I was slowly dying. But that all changed in April. I sold the condo in Jersey City, moved out of the Philly apartment into a five-bedroom, four-bathroom house in South Jersey. We were putting down roots. And I found out I was pregnant again. What a bittersweet moment. On one hand I was happy to be pregnant, but on the other, and in the forefront of my mind, I was thinking, "Will I be able to keep this one?"

This time, I took no chances. I would do no appearances. I would take it easy. And everything was going well. I was in my fourth month and everything was going well. The baby was kicking and I shared every movement and joy with my listeners. I was starting to feel the excitement.

One weekend my sister and niece were visiting and we went outlet shopping in South Jersey. We shopped for household items and things, preparing for the baby. We ended up at my local Shop Rite because I had a craving for a roast beef sub and they made it just the way I liked it. While standing at the counter, waiting for them to make it, I started feeling a sharp pain. I didn't want to say anything because I didn't want to start any shit. This was my neighborhood Shop Rite. People there knew me as Wendy from the radio. I didn't want to be embarrassed. I didn't want to alarm my sister or my niece. I didn't want to create a scene. This is so typical of me—yesterday, today and tomorrow. I don't want to put people out. I don't want to alarm people.

I was feeling these pains and didn't know why. I got my sub and we went back to my home. I mentioned something in passing to my sister who said that it sounds like Braxton Hicks contractions, false alarm, nothing to worry about. It was getting late, so my sister and niece headed back to their home. I put my feet up and I ate my sandwich.

But with each passing minute, I was feeling more and more

pain. Kevin was in New York handling his business. It was about nine in the evening and I was home alone. I was getting worried, but I wasn't too alarmed or thinking about losing the baby. Last time, my water broke. I checked and there was no water and no blood. So I just lay down and started crying. I was going through my emotional thing. I was alone and I was scared. I was in the dreaded fifth month. And I didn't want to call the ambulance and I didn't call my husband because I didn't want him racing down the turnpike, especially for a false alarm. But as the pain increased, I knew I had to do something. So I did break down and call Kevin.

He made it home in forty-five minutes for a commute that normally took an hour and fifteen minutes. I knew I had to get to a hospital and I didn't want to go in an ambulance. I collected my emotions and by the time Kevin got home I was calm. We went to the hospital and they checked me in. I was put in this large, luxurious room. When I had my miscarriage before I was in a tiny room and people kept coming by asking for an autograph. This time I was in a private room with a big cedar closet. It seemed like the type of room they would put someone like Diana Ross if she were having a baby. So I called it the Diana Ross suite.

When I called my parents I was even joking about how they had me in the Diana Ross suite. I was trying to keep everyone's spirits up. Friends were dropping by bringing me food. I had steak and lobster in the Diana Ross suite. Kevin brought my makeup, my hair piece, my fluffy slippers and favorite robe. One of the reasons why I love him is that he knows me—he knows how I love to look and what makes me feel good.

I was yukking it up in the Diana Ross suite. All the time I had no idea we were actually going to lose another baby. I was in the hospital approximately a week and the doctors forced delivery. The baby was dead inside me the entire week. I didn't want to know the sex of the baby this time. But a nurse came in and said, "You had a girl." *Did I ask you?!* As long as that was out of the bag, I asked the nurse how she was. She told me she was discolored and polluted. It was terrible. Once again we opted not to have a formal funeral. I wanted to leave that hospital and start over again and leave all of that pain and despair right there.

On the way out of the hospital they make you ride in a wheelchair. And one of the nurses handed me a hospital folder, which I assumed was the bill with all of the charges from my stay. I opened it and it was the records of my baby girl, including her little footprints.

I dumped the entire folder in the garbage at the curb near our car. I didn't want that kind of memory. I wanted nothing. They asked me if I wanted to name her. I told them no. She would simply join her sister in heaven and they will both be there waiting for me when I get there.

By the next week I was back on the radio again. And once again I had to explain to my radio community how I lost another baby. Shit happens. And they say that in life much rain must fall and what doesn't kill you only makes you stronger. Well, fuck that. It's easy to say but until you go through something like that . . .

well, let's just say I wasn't seeing all the silver lining at that point. I wanted to die.

Hey, didn't I do the right thing? I got off drugs. I was clean. I was living right. Hell, I had even gotten married. I made all of my doctors' appointments. I was taking it easy. And it didn't matter. I went through the pain of feeling a baby grow inside of me. I felt her kick and move. We sang to her and talked to her every night. Everything was so right. And everything was going so wrong. Four months before she was to make an appearance in this world we lost her. Gone. Pain. I said to myself, "Well, I guess everyone can't have everything."

Losing babies. To me it doesn't compare to losing loved ones. At least people who have been here had a chance to live. You got a chance to experience them, get to know them, get to really love them. But losing a baby is like being stripped of the opportunity to love something you created.

I felt so hollow. I felt like a woman with everything but the thing she wanted the most. I felt like I was failing my husband. And at that point I was thinking that perhaps getting a divorce would probably be the best thing. I knew I'd be a mother. I was not opposed to adoption. I figured I would be a single parent, adopt a beautiful girl or boy. But first I would divorce Kevin. I was in such pain not just because I lost the babies but also because I failed him.

Here I have this near-perfect guy, with so much life and so young and here I am, damaged and cannot give him a child. I've tied down a man who could go off and have children with a perfect woman but he's married to me. If we weren't married he could just pick up and move on and have that family. I felt he deserved to have children. And I was not sure if I could ever give him any. Why should he suffer through life never having a child to carry on his genes and family name? I wasn't going to do that to him. And mind you, Kevin never pressured me about having kids. In fact he was a real trooper. He would say in his cute, thug way, "Baby, it doesn't matter. We don't need a baby. We can just spend our time spoiling each other."

But I wasn't buying that. I felt at that point, I would just release him. Let him go and find a woman who could bear him a child.

I recall thinking heavily about divorce and not talking to anyone. At the same time I was trying to pull it all together and get on with my life. Three days after being released from the hospital I decided I would go to the mall. I got out of bed, put on my makeup, did my hair, put on my designer clothes, threw on a fur, got in one of my new Mercedes Benzes and headed for the mall. When I got to the first light, I just broke down and started crying, right there. I looked to my left and there was a little girl in the passenger seat looking over at me. I had on my Christian Dior shades and I know I must have looked like so many ladies I used to see when I was a little girl riding in my mother's car. I used to see the ladies at the light, in the designer shades, driving an expensive, luxury car, with that "rich" look and think to myself, "I'm going to be like that when I grow up." She was so fabulous. I aspired to become the lady at the traffic light.

I just never knew that the woman at the red light could have so much pain and so many tears behind those designer shades—that was until I became the lady at the light. Perhaps that lady back then was hiding so much like I was that day. Maybe she used a lot of Visine to hide her red, tear-stained eyes. Maybe she, too, used cold compresses to keep down the puffiness under her eyes. Maybe the lady that I admired so much as a little girl was no happier with her life than I was in mine.

And I had to go through this pain alone. The deepest, deepest pains of a woman I don't think men understand. I wasn't going to burden Kevin with it. My mom and dad would understand, but I didn't want her flying up here to be mom. My sister and brother had their own lives. I didn't want to burden them. And I think all of that doting and hand-holding makes the healing process that much slower. I didn't want that. I wanted to heal fast. So I shared with the only people I could share with at this time—my listeners. This was my second five-month miscarriage. And I was amazed by the number of faxes and calls I got from all over Delaware Valley of women telling me they went through or were going through the same thing. I thought, "Why weren't people talking about this before?" People talk as if having a baby is so damned easy.

I know four different couples right now who are having trouble having a baby who are seeing specialists. If having babies is no problem for you, please know that you are blessed. Because there are too many for whom the experience is most difficult.

Between the two five-month miscarriages, I got hit with

another whammy. My doctors found that I had thyroid disease. They said it could come from a number of things, including stress (and I had plenty of that). My parents kept asking me why I was talking with my eyes popped out and sweating all the damn time (and at this time I had stopped using coke). I went to the doctor and he discovered a lump, a goiter in my throat area. They treated it by making me drink a radiation drink that burned out my thyroid and put me on medication which regulated my system, replacing the duties of the thyroid. I have to take a pill every day for the rest of my life to keep my system regulated. So I'm dealing with all of this and trying to stay strong.

Mother's Day 1999 rolled around and it was the saddest day of my life. I spent the day reflecting on what might have been and how empty and sad I was. At this point I changed my shopping hours to a time when I thought few kids would be in the stores. I couldn't bear to see any kids.

Fast-forward to November of 1999. I had this strong urge to get some sushi. I got some takeout from the sushi place not too far from our home. I pulled out of the parking lot feeling real crazy. I was very cloudy and I pulled out right in front of another car and it sideswiped my shiny Mercedes, which was sitting on 22s. And while I was thinking, "Oh, shit, what am I going to tell Kevin" (you know how niggas are about their cars)—I was also thinking, "I really feel weird."

I exchanged info with the guy who hit me and I headed home, thinking all the way that I needed to come up with a good story for how this had happened because I did not want to hear Kevin's mouth. I decided to tell him that I thought I was pregnant (because somewhere inside I thought I was). I stopped off on the way home and got an EPT. I went home, took the test and in three minutes that little strip came up pink. I was pregnant.

All I could think was, "I am pregnant and I'm not going to be screamed on about the car."

I was pregnant. Again.

I told Kevin about the car and the pregnancy and he was excited. We made an appointment to see a doctor the next day and confirmed everything. And what we also found out was that if I was going to actually have this baby, I needed to have a cerclage and bed rest. They discovered that the reason why I kept losing my babies was because my cervix was weak and couldn't support the weight of the baby. I told the job about the baby in my third month, which was when I got the cerclage and was put on bed rest. The station was very understanding. I put them on notice—no appearances. Thanks to modern technology, they hooked up a mike in my home and every morning I went to work from my bed. The doctor said I could be on my feet no longer than thirty minutes a day. I reduced that to fifteen minutes—again, not taking any chances. I got up long enough to go to the bathroom, basically, and that was it. Oh, and if I had doctors' appointments, I would get up for that. I had two doctors' visits a week—one with my regular GYN and another with a specialist. I enjoyed going to the doctor because every week I got confirmation that I was still pregnant and the baby was fine. The specialist gave me an ultrasound every visit where I could see the baby and hear the heart beat. So I looked forward to my doctors' visits.

I had a contraction monitor in my home. And no friends visited. I didn't want to burden them. Kevin set up a cooler next to the bed and before he would leave for work every morning he made sure I had enough to eat and drink for the day. So I lay in bed after work and ordered everything I could think of from QVC—everything but baby clothes (I wasn't doing that again). I would order scarves, potpourri, Suzanne Somers pajamas . . . anything and everything. I was addicted to QVC. I watched hours and hours of television and would change the channel when babies appeared. I didn't want to come to terms with what I was going through. I was pregnant and I couldn't go through another tragedy.

Kevin and I decided we were going to do everything in our power to make sure we kept this baby. We decided there would be no sex. Not because the doctor ordered it, but that's what we elected to do. We did not want to do anything to agitate the area. When I say no sex, I mean no orgasms. Not even a blow job because, well, that would agitate the area because it would make me aroused. I wasn't taking any chances.

And with this pregnancy, there would be no fights. It's not something we talked about; it's just the way it was. I talked in nice tones; he talked in nice tones.

We had a housekeeper. And we hired an assistant who would run errands like doing the grocery shopping and picking up clothes from the cleaners. There was nothing for me to do but watch TV, shop and eat. I was eating anything I ever wanted to eat. There were no limits. And by my eighth month, I had ballooned. I was a blob. I had gained more than one hundred pounds. Nearing my ninth month, they also cut my cerclage. It was a signal that I was ready and all systems were go for delivery.

I made them give me the cerclage in a plastic baggy. Hell no, I didn't want them to throw it out because I'm nasty and sentimental. They used this thick shit that looked like whale stitching. It was very nasty. But I wanted it. It was a reminder of what I went through to get to that point. It was mine. Nobody will ever understand. Maybe one day, I'll show it to my nasty son when he gets older and tell him, "This is the difference between you being here and not being here." It's in my freezer today waiting for him.

Oh, yeah, I gave birth . . . to a perfect, healthy baby boy. On August 18, 2000—my beautiful baby arrived, one week overdue. Kevin Samuel (named for my "papa," my late maternal grandfather) Hunter was seven pounds, twenty ounces, nineteen and a half inches long. He had ten fingers and ten toes. He was perfect.

I had him the old-fashioned way—I pushed, pushed, pushed. I blew my insides out. The delivery took forty-five minutes—I did it like a champ. Yes, I had an epidural. I might have gotten three of them as much pain as I was in.

Kevin was right there the whole time. And it felt good. I was so glad he wasn't a "baby's daddy." There's nothing like delivering a baby with your "husband" there holding your hand through the whole process. There is a sense of endearment you feel for your man during that time that can't be explained. And I was so grateful that this was the first time he was experiencing this. I always knew I didn't want the drama of dealing with a man with kids. But I never understood the deeper meaning of that feeling until I put on my own baby show for him. It was a special moment made even more special because we both shared it together for the first time.

And I delivered him a son. Shout-outs to all the women who delivered beautiful baby girls. They are blessings, too. But the men, they want a son. The bastards! They might not admit it to you. But men want sons. They want someone cut in their own cloth. Women, we will love any sex. But men want that child in their image. And I delivered him his very own little Kevin, Kevin Jr.

After they brought him to me all cleaned up, I never let him go. I slept with him in my arms for twenty-four hours. My husband was exhausted and slept in the chair next to us. Everybody came through—my parents, our friends, his mother—all bringing things, champagne, cigars, flowers. And when the party was over my baby was still with me, clutched in my arms. I had pains in my arm muscles from holding him so tight. I had never held a baby before. Isn't that strange? In all my years, I had never held a baby until I held my own. I was scared to hold my niece or nephew when they were babies.

Even growing up I wasn't one of those girly girls. I didn't play with Barbie dolls and dream about having a baby of my own. I wasn't a tomboy; I just wasn't all that maternal. Prior to having my own baby, I was the woman in Bloomingdale's who looked at the mothers with their screaming kids and thought to myself, "Oh brother, get these kids out of the way. Can't you see I'm shopping!" In my mind, I could give a damn. I didn't even baby-sit much when I was growing up. If I did the kid was about nine or ten—no babies. And I was doing it strictly for the money, not because I loved being around kids.

Holding little Kevin was my first experience with maternal feelings and it was the most joyous feeling I have ever had. I was never letting him go. Even when Nurse Ratchet came to get him circumcised, I rolled myself out of bed and carried him to the operating room. I wasn't letting them do anything to my baby without me being there to watch. They might try to switch my baby on me. I watch Lifetime, I see what goes on. We worked too hard to have him for anything like that to happen.

The next day we went home. It was the scariest drive we ever had. We drove from the hospital in Philly to our home in South Jersey on the shoulder with the flashers on. I never asked Kevin to do that. But we must have been on the same wavelength because I was thinking the same thing. He drove on the shoulder, with his seat up. Now if you've ever seen a thug drive a car, you know he has to have the seat all the way back, practically in the back seat, with that lean. But Kevin had his seat up, and he was all hugged up on the steering wheel. And the radio was off. I sat in the back seat staring at our son. I was in love and speechless and couldn't stop my tears of joy.

We were so happy and so cautious. You would have thought we were the first couple ever to deliver a baby. When I got home, my mother and father were there with the spread—it was like

Soul Food Sunday. My mother loves to cook and she made everything from scratch. My father, brother, sister and brother-in-law were all there cooing and catering to me. I was like queen for the day. A queen and her prince. I was in heaven.

I had made a deal with God entering my ninth month and I realized I had put on about one hundred and five pounds that if I had this baby I would not obsess about losing the weight and greet my baby with a smile. I even told God I would drive a minivan if I had to. "Lord, I will drive a minivan for you!"

The weight? Well, while I was in my eighth month, I scheduled a tummy tuck for four months after my delivery. And I traded in my Lexus 470 jeep for a minivan. It was a Mercedes ML-500 AMG. Don't get it twisted, people, that particular Mercedes is a minivan. So don't go putting rims on it because you can't really dress up a minivan. It is what it is.

I got my minivan. I had my husband. I had my career. And I finally got my baby. Everything was perfect. But things are not exactly what they appear. In the midst of all of this joy, yet another seed of turmoil found a way to root itself in my life.

CHAPTER 12

It Is What It Is

THE BABY WAS ONE MONTH OLD and I was trying to get back to normal, which was very hard considering that I had gained more than one hundred pounds during my pregnancy. I lost six pounds but my body was a mess. I was looking forward to going back to work—which was still weeks away—and feeling good about myself again.

One evening, Kevin's cell phone was ringing. It was two o'clock in the morning. That wasn't unusual because in the game we're in, business doesn't really jump off until the wee hours. Actually, business gets done twenty-four hours a day. That phone call could have been someone calling from The Tunnel, a New York City nightclub, saying some rapper just left the club and careened off the West Side Highway and this was info that I could have needed when I crack the mike at five o'clock. Cell phones stay on because you never know. Two o'clock here is just eleven in Los Angeles and some shit could have just jumped off that I need for my show. So it wasn't unusual for the cell phone to ring.

Kevin looked at it and ignored it the first time. It rang about twenty seconds later and Kevin picked it up and hung up. That was a little unusual. It rang again. He did the same thing. It kept ringing and finally he picked up the phone and left the room. Now it wasn't unusual for him to take the phone into the bathroom. Kevin has a very Ja-Rule-esq, gravelly voice that's loud even when he's trying to whisper, even when he's being pleasant. So he would often take the phone into the bathroom so as not to disturb me. But he took the phone and went to the guest bedroom on the other side of the house. Now that was unusual and made me get up to find out what the fuck was going on.

I got out of bed and followed him quietly to the guest bedroom. I was curious. And I had no idea. I swear to God I had no idea. I stood in the doorway and listened for a few seconds before I got an idea. I don't remember the content of the conversation but all I remember is Kevin saying this woman's name. It was a nasty conversation, one of these "bitch-please!" conversations. And he said her name. Mind you, my husband is not the kind to call someone by their first name. Ever. He oftentimes calls me "Yo" or one of the affectionate names he has for me.

For him to be calling another woman by her name led me to believe that this person was closer than just a business associate. There was something deeper going on. *Well, duh!* This was a bitch and they were arguing. I must have stood there and listened to about forty-five seconds of that conversation before I walked in and snatched the cell phone out of his hand.

"What the fuck is going on?" I said in a nasty low growl. I

didn't want to wake up the baby so I tried to keep it down. But I felt like I was having an out-of-body experience. I felt like whatever he said, I *knew* what the fuck was going on. In those forty-five seconds my woman's intuition kicked in and I knew he was on the phone with a lover.

I felt hurt. I felt like a fool for asking what the fuck was going on. And I felt totally out of my mind. Nothing had prepared me for this. No matter how many Jerry Springer or Ricki Lake shows I saw, no matter how many *Cosmo* articles I read, nothing prepared me for this. Nothing.

And from the time I asked that stupid question until he actually parted his lips to answer seemed like an eternity. But actually he answered right away. He spilled the beans. I didn't talk to the girl; I hung up on her because I knew the affair was his fault. He's the married man with a child. He could have said no to the affair.

I took the phone and threw it over the staircase to the first floor. Now somehow I had the presence of mind not to throw the phone out the window. I didn't want to pay for a new window. I didn't throw it against the walls because gouges in the wall are not cool. I didn't want to break the Lladro or the china and crystal I have throughout the house. I was angry and I wanted to the throw the phone but I wasn't going to wreck my home and somewhere I knew I wanted to keep the phone intact because I wanted to retrieve the numbers—that's why I didn't throw it in the toilet, either.

Yes, I know it's abnormal to think like that. But my abnormality is one of my best features. My way of thinking. I can't even explain it to people. But I managed to throw the phone over the balcony of the top floor, aiming for the plush carpet below—not the marble hallway.

I started crying. I don't recall exactly what he said but I remember looking into his eyes—those eyes again—and a part of me believing every word out of his mouth. He was talking about being stressed out and needing an outlet. And how she didn't mean anything to him. He told me the details about their relationship, how it started and how it was a very callous type situation and physically she was holding him down during the time I couldn't. And somewhere in me I hated myself for understanding. How could I understand some bullshit like that? But a man has needs and I couldn't do shit. I couldn't even suck his dick. I was literally this big fat blob lying in the bed waiting to have a baby. Who could blame him, the sick bitch inside my head said.

I'm seeing him throughout the pregnancy having to hold his tongue. Before we would have knock-down drag-outs. We go to the wall with our arguments. But for nine months this man—who has a nasty temper and says exactly what's on his mind—was sweet as sugar. And during this time he's driving up and down the New Jersey Turnpike, notorious for racial profiling. And he just happens to fit the profile—thug guy in a nice ride. Men like my man are public enemy number one to many cops on the turnpike. And I was lying in the bed back at home, useless, while he was out there holding it down for us, taking care of his business.

Kevin started managing me part-time when we were in Philly. He would book some guests and handle some of my appearances before I got pregnant. When I was pregnant and on bed rest, he even arranged for Lisa (Left Eye) Lopes to come to the house for a live interview. She came with her boyfriend at the time. And while the studio was doing their thing they would cut to me and Left Eye from my home. It was a great interview. She was very gracious.

Kevin was also going to the clubs and making sure I had the A-list rappers on my show. Philly is not New York and to get an A-list rapper to roll through early in the morning in Philly was like pulling teeth.

Was there a lot of pressure on him? Yes. Did he need a release? Probably. Part of me understood this. The other part knew he needed to find a better release and a better damn excuse than this sorry one.

But being in the gossip world, I was also all too familiar with beautiful women who were cheated on for less. The most beautiful women in the world—Halle Berry (her man talking about being a sex addict), Janet Jackson, allegedly J. Lo—hell I was in damn good company. What makes me so special?

But after I thought about it, I came to the conclusion that I *am* special and I didn't deserve this. No woman deserves this. And I hated him, with every fiber in my body. And I wanted to kill him. I mean really kill him. For real. I wanted to kill him more because I was in the process of breaking my Number One Rule: No Cheating. Cheat and I'm gone. I wanted to kill him because I still loved him and didn't want to leave him. I was angry about that. And the excuse was lame. My husband is one of the strongest-willed people I know. How could he have gotten weak for the flesh? How could he betray me? How could he betray us?

I know other niggas who wanted to look and holla at me and I never gave any of them as much as a second look. When it came to sex with my husband, I'm down for whatever. I mean, Kevin couldn't find a more willing partner. I was out of commission for about nine months. Didn't he know that the situation was temporary? How could he do this to me? How could he do this to me?

I hired a private detective. I had to know who she was on some other level. At this point the shit was over, which was why she was calling so much. But I needed to know if she was in love? Was he in love? Were condoms used? Is she pregnant? Was she laying up in the Marriott with him? I don't want to disrespect her and go into the details of the answers but let's just say I was satisfied with all the answers that I got.

I realize that this might be an open forum to shout out her name and disrespect her. It's not like I have a lot of respect for a woman who wrecks a home. I don't have a lot of respect for a woman who sleeps with a man she knows is married with a child. I don't respect her but I'm a big enough woman not to disrespect her. She is a nonentity in our lives. And I've learned so much from that experience. I have just moved on. We have moved on.

I've matured and I'm trying to set an example for other women who go through this situation. Don't pick the low road wanting to beat a bitch's ass and put up signs all around her workplace and call up her mother, and all of that drama. You have to deal with your man because ultimately it's your man's fault. Plenty of women out there are trifling. But if the man gives in, then it's the man's fault; that's why I'm taking the high road and not disrespecting her.

I have tried to understand why he cheated. I understand that sometimes a man just needs a vessel and you can take that for what it is. In the long run that was the release that he needed in order for him to come to me laid up in the bed with smiles even at the end of a fucked-up day when receipts come up short because muthafuckas are ripping him off—because the streets are ugly. At the end of the day he would come to me with a roast beef sandwich and a smile. If that's what he needed to do to come to me with smiles, sing to my baby, and come to me with pleasant tones, I'll take that.

The part of me that wanted to kill him lost to the part of me that loved him and understood him.

He explained that it was one girl. I knew her name. I asked him a million questions. After I found out why he did it, I spent weeks being in deep hate and anger toward him. But I thought, "Better to happen now, when I really have to fight for a relationship." I know it sounds crazy.

It happened at a time when I couldn't just bail. As you know from my first marriage I will bail if things aren't right. I will bail on friendships if they aren't going right. I will just bail if I don't like the way things are going down. But during this period while the baby was brand-new I was in no condition to be a single mother, mentally or physically. Physically, being a hundred pounds overweight I really didn't feel like I could go back on the market. I didn't feel like a swarm of men would be stepping over each other to get to me. Nothing makes a woman feel good like being sought after by a bunch of men.

I was a new mother and did not know how to be a mother. I was so confused. I was so lost. And for lack of a better way of saying it, I was stuck with Kevin until I could get myself together. By the time I got myself together physically and emotionally, Kevin and I were back together and mentally in sync. So as far as the affair is concerned, it was the first time it had ever happened to me (that I know of) and it was the best time for it to happen to me because I could not bail like I'm prone to do.

I'm glad for that because Kevin and I are a stronger couple today. And I am a better mother. This happening at this time forced me to focus on my son. My being a mother kept me sane for my baby. If I wasn't a new mother I might have dove back into cocaine and lost my mind. If I did not gain a hundred pounds I might have cheated on him to get him back. And if I cheated, I was not cheating with any old dude, I would cheat grandiose— the way I do everything. I'm talking about picking up Allen Iverson or some other famous, sexy man. You have got to cut him where it hurts. If you're going to cut him, cut him good. So when he finds out about your affair you can let him know that he cheated with a ho and you cheated with Denzel.

I wanted to stand by my convictions and leave him. But I couldn't. We have a son and his name is Kevin Hunter. And my name is Wendy Hunter. I wasn't ready to make that move.

Kevin and I were never separated and we never slept in separate bedrooms through the whole ordeal. I believe if you're going to be in it, you're going to be in it. Separations are just free passes to bone whoever you want. You set up your bachelorette apartment and he sets up his bachelor's apartment and then what? You all get back together in six months? The separation business only drains your pockets and further strains the relationship. Either you're married (for better or worse) or you get a divorce.

And no one should sleep on the couch. You can sleep with your back to each other and don't touch. But you're either married or divorced. For me, there's no in-between. You either love him or you hate him. My emotions either run hot or cold. I'm not a lukewarm person. Either I'm going to cut off all of my hair or I'm going to have it growing down to my butt crack. There is no in-between.

Sure, I gave Kevin the silent treatment and, yes, there were plenty of ice-cold nights with my back to him. Maybe we didn't speak for days. But I was a mother to my son and he was a father to his son. We somehow worked it out.

Somewhere in Kevin's soulful eyes—those eyes that I looked into on our first date and knew this was one sincere man—I saw that this could be repaired. When a man hurts a good woman and if he's really a good man he knows what he has done. Shit happens.

He was racing up and down the turnpike doing his part while I'm in bed worried about losing another baby. And guess what? That's on his mind, too. All he knows is he's got to be there and strong for his woman. If that's what it took at that particular time (and I stress *that particular time* because cheating is not acceptable), then I'll take that, too. If that's what it took for him to come to me . . . then all is forgiven. Not forgotten. But forgiven.

In order to be able to close the chapter, I had to find out more about her though. I know my man enough to know what he will and will not do. I know him enough to know that if certain things are happening with the situation, I'll know just how deep it got. I needed to know whether he secretly had another baby somewhere. It would be very easy for him to have two families with me in South Jersey and him in North Jersey all the time. I had to do my own investigations. I *had* to know.

And the way I physically looked was affecting the way I felt. That he had an affair and I was not able to confidently whip off my clothes and whip it on him was driving me crazy. And then to cap that with the baby—I didn't even know how to take care of a baby and was just doing the best I could and wondering if that was enough. Then I have a job where I have to get up at four in the morning. All that and I have a group of friends who would do nothing but gossip from one to the other if I told them about any of it. I was a mess.

And get this, the one person who I could actually talk to—the one person who I needed to talk to, my very best friend, was the person who hurt me the most. I was in unfamiliar waters with this one. I just didn't know what to do. It would have been easier if I was getting a divorce. I could just tell everybody what the muthafucka did and be done with it. But I was staying and I felt like a fool. I'm my own fool and I didn't want to be judged. I hired a private detective because I needed closure.

The very phone that I threw down the stairs I retrieved that night and jotted down the number that was in there ten times. I didn't know what I was going to do with the number but I knew I needed it. I had her first name and a phone number and I gave that to the private detective. I found him in the Yellow Pages.

I needed to know who this woman was in order to get over this hurdle. And the only thing that would make me walk out for good is if he lied about anything—if he was in love, if she was just as successful at what she does as I am in my career, if she had *his* baby. Please tell me she's a maid at the Marriott—no disrespect to maids—but somehow in there I would feel better about the situation if she was.

Kevin gave me information, but not all that I was asking for. There were certain things that I wanted to know on my own. He knew me too well. He wouldn't give me her last name or any details. That was okay. Thank God I made enough money to get answers for myself. This was a matter of life and death—his life, his death. The private investigator was willing to fly all over, drive all over and do whatever was needed to get my answers. I had the money and this is what money is used for. This was about my sanity.

A private detective is a wonderful thing. He can find out everything about a person—down to her last period—from a single phone number. He got her home address, her work address, her Social Security number, her last name. He was able to tell me whether she was married and if she had kids. He even broke down her living situation for me. He did all of this in thirty days. And it cost me about eight hundred dollars. A very small price to pay for my sanity.

I knew I had to pay a visit to this woman. I had no idea what I would do when I saw her. I didn't know how I was going see her. But I knew I would. Part of me knew that going to see her was childish. I knew ultimately Kevin's decision to cheat was on Kevin. But the other part didn't give a damn about that. This woman fucked my husband knowing he was my husband. He told her who I was. He told her that I was pregnant and couldn't have sex. She knew what was going on. To me, you can explain to a woman all day long and they can pretend to be in it just for the sex but women are soft and pink. At the end of the day, women—and I don't care what they say—want more. On December 25, they're not looking just for a gift; they're looking for your time. You cannot carry on a relationship with a married man and not be jealous of the main woman. I was the main woman. I am the wife. And the wife gets everything.

I was trying to save our marriage and I was out of my head with loneliness and with the empty feeling of betrayal. I was out of my fucking head.

So one morning after I got off my shift at ten, I made that trip north up the New Jersey Turnpike in a rented car. I did not want to be in a recognizable vehicle and I didn't know if she had been in our vehicles. It was a very white-knuckle drive. I was furious the whole ride, which seemed to just fly by. I had The Club with me, the antitheft device I'd borrowed from my car, just in case we fought. I had never been in a fistfight before but I knew I needed some backup if did get in one.

I decided to wait for her at her job. I got to her office and watched her leave her building. I knew what she looked like because my private detective had gotten to her office building and somehow gotten into a superficial conversation with her. He took a picture of her with a secret camera. I watched her leave the building from my parked rental car. I never approached her.

What was I going to get out of approaching her? A fistfight, probably. That would mean that she got to me. My ultimate goal was to save my family. I loved my husband and I needed to feel like I had personal closure as a woman, closure that he could not give me. As a woman I needed to know what she looked like in person. Where does she work? Is she a secretary or is she the boss of the whole shit? What does she drive, if she drives at all? Does she weigh a hundred and five pounds or three hundred and five pounds? You want to know all these things. I was satisfied with what I saw and ultimately speaking, I won. I wasn't there to fight her. I was there to fight myself emotionally and fight to save my family. And I won. I maintained my sobriety through this whole ordeal. I thought I might end up being a single mother and I needed to be on point. I did not think about picking up a drink, a joint, coke or anything. I was fueled by anger. And I didn't want to run away from this, I needed to confront it.

This was a bump in our road. Ultimately speaking it has made us a stronger couple. It's hard to say, but my husband is a better man because of this. I'm a better woman, a better wife and a better mother. I'm a better friend. I'm a better radio personality because I relate now to the women who call up and talk about how their man cheated on them. Kevin never knew what I did that day (until now). It's not something I could explain.

Since being back in New York, she hasn't contacted me. One of the apprehensions I had about coming back to New York, in a market where she lives, was having to relive Kevin's past mistake and wonder if this woman would jump up and cause problems for us. It hasn't happened. And this is why I'm not talking about her in terrible terms. No, it's not that I respect her. And no, it's not that I like her. She is a nonentity in my mind. She is my husband's mistake. And this is my forgiveness and that's the way it is.

I feel after going through that in a weird way it's made me and Kevin a strong unit. And it's made me a strong woman. I don't know what the future holds but the reality of betrayal by my best friend has brought to the forefront a lot of realities of life that I wasn't familiar with before. But I can honestly say the wound has been healed.

We both keep late hours hustling the streets doing what we have to do for the betterment of our family. When my husband keeps late hours and I'm not with him—because I'm a mother and a wife and queen of the radio and I have to take care of myself—I do not worry about where he is. When he pulls in at four in the morning, my mind does not dwell on what bitch is he fucking. I'm not worried that he's coming from some woman's house. I am thankful that he was not racially profiled that night and made it home safely.

He knows the deal. And so do I. There are men who learn from their mistakes and my husband is one of them. There are men who deserve forgiveness and there are marriages that can survive betrayals. And I never thought about cheating on him as a way to get back at him. What would that prove? That would prove to my son that I'm a whore. That I am some sort of whore.

There is a double standard. Men can cheat and come back from it. When women do it, we are branded all kinds of things. I accept that, too. So I chose to believe him, trust him. And I chose to stay. I don't know any men who can put it down the way my husband does. I don't mean just physically. I mean all around. He is a special man. I love him to death despite his mistakes. We've moved on. My husband made a mistake. But I never questioned his love for me. He's mine. I won.

CHAPTER 13

Kevin's Side

KEVIN: I'm going to be honest. I never pictured myself being married. Neither one of us was on the marriage tip when we met. I think Wendy was even more apprehensive because of all that went down with her first marriage. I know she was looking at me and saying, "What is this nigga about?" She could tell I was a certain kind of a dude, very different from the kind of man she had been with in the past. And she just wasn't interested in getting married again.

I wasn't feeling marriage either because I've never seen too many that actually work. I don't know too many people who are really good at the marriage thing. They never seem to last. And you can talk about years invested and all that but everybody I knew, marriage didn't work for them. Maybe they got bored with each other or maybe the finances weren't right. Whatever the reason, it just didn't work.

Yeah, so with all of that, somehow Wendy and I ended up at the altar.

WENDY: The emotional strain of having a baby was taking its toll.

KEVIN: And I felt like I had to show Wendy that no matter what, that I wasn't going anywhere. I love Wendy dearly and I was there one hundred and fifty percent for her. But to be honest losing the babies was wearing on me, too. I tried to shield her from ever seeing me break down. I needed to be strong for her all of the time.

But I wasn't strong all the time. You know, when you're going after everything you think you want and you can't attain those things—not even through hard work. It's very hard to be up against something that no matter what you do—hard work or whatever—it just ain't happening. It was very tough. It was depressing and it was difficult at times to take. But all I ever wanted Wendy to see in me was strength. I never wanted her to see me going through it. I never wanted Wendy to see me weak—not weak as in crying and all of that. Just weak.

I'm a strong individual. I've been on my own since I was seventeen years old when my mother gave me a choice to abide by her rules and not stay out late and go to school or get out. I got out. And I struggled. I hustled to create a way for myself. I started my own business and when I met Wendy I didn't come to the table with nothing—I had my own. So I have endured a lot and been through a lot. But this was one time in my life when I felt like I really wanted something and couldn't get it and I couldn't explain why. It didn't have anything to do with our love. I just felt like God didn't want us to have this. After everything we'd done and been through, God just didn't want us to have a baby. And I couldn't understand why.

So I felt a little dirty. I felt that within myself I needed to do certain things to feel like more of a man. I'm not going to lie. During this trying time certain things happened. I'm a man. I'm not perfect.

WENDY: I had my questions as most women do but in a weird kind of way. I tell women that infidelity's not necessarily a reason to get divorced. He and I were married and we were struggling to have a baby. And—I'll put it bluntly—I couldn't have sex. I had already had three miscarriages—two at five months, one at seven weeks and I couldn't have sex during the last pregnancy.

KEVIN: The sex wasn't really the reason why I did what I did. I needed to have an outlet. I was slightly vulnerable and it just happened. It wasn't a big thing. It wasn't a big thing to me. It wasn't a thing where I lied and said a bunch of shit to try to get Shorty, to try and persuade her to do that. I said, "Don't think that I'm going to do a whole bunch of spectacular shit for you. I'm going through a little thing right now. I have a wife, this is who she is and this is what it's going to be." And she was down with that. I just needed an outlet.

This is a touchy subject and I need to just tell it the way I see it. We need to air this out. This is like a cleansing.

As far as respect. She wasn't a foul type of chick who was looking for exposure or something more than what I was willing to give. Sixty percent of the women who I know who pat

Wendy on the back and tell her how much they love her and all that would love to be able to say to her on the back end, "You think your man is all of that . . . well listen to this. I fucked him! All that shit you talking and I fucked him."

But Shorty wasn't like that. She knew who Wendy was and never tried to go there.

Give me some credit, too. The type of guy that I am, regardless of what I did, would not allow any woman to just play me like that. A large part of why she didn't is because I don't carry myself like that. People know how far to go with me. I wouldn't say it's fear, just respect. I was very up-front: "This is what it is and this is how it's going down."

Men seem to be able to separate love from sex. For me the affair was not that serious. It's serious when it becomes a long, drawn-out thing and you're dealing with somebody who doesn't understand. It only becomes serious when feelings get involved. If you know you're involved in a situation and you're married and you are up-front that you have no intentions on leaving your wife and this ain't no "love thing," then it's not serious.

WENDY: But that kind of situation can only last for a little while before it turns serious for the woman. After a certain threshold women start to want more—no matter what kind of parameters have been set by the man.

KEVIN: Because of the bond that Wendy and I have it wasn't meant for me to carry on a long-standing relationship with another woman. I guess there was some divine intervention.

Little things were happening that tipped Wendy off that made absolutely no sense.

WENDY: I have an aunt Joan who died the year before I was born. My name is Wendy Joan. She was thirty and I always feel like aunt Joan is my liaison to God. God is too busy to watch all of us so every one of us has a representative. My one representative is my aunt Joan. And she only alerts God when it's something really big. Otherwise she handles all of the business for Him on my behalf.

I think she handled this cheating thing on my behalf. She tipped me off on a few things Kevin was up to.

KEVIN: It was very important to me that I shield Wendy from any hurt. I was going to great lengths to make sure she would never find out. But somehow, she kept finding out things and all I could say was, "How the fuck did she know that? This aunt Joan. She's up there fucking up my flow!"

I wasn't out there trying to hurt anybody. I was just trying to get a little peace of mind because I knew when I went back to the crib I would have to be ultra strong and endure a lot.

Not to say that Wendy was a total bitch at the time because she's not like that. But having a baby was a trying, emotional period for both of us. It was a very sensitive time and I needed to be able to handle it. I had to be strong. I couldn't be one of these weak niggas and act like I couldn't handle this shit because I've been blessed with such a good woman and a lot of good things have been happening so maybe this was God's test. Maybe He was saying, "You inherited a nice situation with a nice woman." (Now, I deserved it. It's not like I got lucky.) "But let's see if you can sustain through a real storm. Y'all have been living real rosy. Now here's the stormy part."

I didn't want to fail that part. But I felt like if I didn't have a vehicle to release then I would burst. In my circles and how I have to move I don't have time to bowl or play ball or do the stuff other dudes do to release.

WENDY: And his friends didn't know about this girl.

KEVIN: And being hot with this shit—being popular off the strength of Wendy as well as living a certain lifestyle—will attract a lot of negativity as well as positivity. It all started dipping a little bit. That's no excuse though. Yeah, there were other outlets I should have taken.

WENDY: He exercises those other outlets now.

KEVIN: I don't bowl now or anything like that. I talk to Wendy now when things get heated. We're a realistic couple now. Since that happened—and I know this sounds crazy—we're much closer as a couple. A part of me needed to see if things really went crazy like they did would my woman go all the way out for me. Or is this just a farce or some game.

And she went all out for me. Now I know, "Okay, we can get through all of this." And I know what I have. As well as having a superstar for a wife, I have a realistic partner. I have a down-ass chick.

WENDY: It was ugly emotionally and he can't really answer from a woman's point of view. I never thought that the first time I would experience infidelity, my trial run would be with a man who I am so in love with and now, "What?! I'm a new mother?!" And I'm all confused.

KEVIN: Hold up, hold up.

WENDY: I was more than one hundred pounds overweight. I had a job that I loved (the situation may not have been perfect, but I loved the job). And now I have a new baby. What do I do? I don't know how to be a mother. And now I'm going through this. I knew it wasn't my fault that he was unfaithful. I never blamed myself.

KEVIN: We had a lot invested. We weren't going to just throw it all away. We were going to work it out. She forgave me. And we worked it out. I know there's a double standard. It's a man's world. I know things are slowly changing but it's more accepted when men do certain things. I'm not saying it was right, I'm just saying that's how it is.

If she did the same thing, I would be gone. She doesn't get a free pass. Absolutely not. No free passes.

WENDY: Ironically, I don't want a free pass to cheat. My way of getting back at him had nothing to do with cheating on him. I was not interested in doing that. I didn't want to.

KEVIN: We talked about it like real people . . .

WENDY: . . . I'm not going out like that. Women can call it what they want. But if your man cheats on you and you cheat on him, talking about getting back at him, then you are playing yourself. And I wasn't going out like that.

KEVIN: It got to a point where we sat back and evaluated the situation for what it is. The lifestyle that we lead and the places we have to be, we have to examine things unlike the common man. I had to tell her, "It happened. It was what it was. I don't love Shorty. We did this . . ." I had to go through the question-and-answer period.

WENDY: Yeah, like, "Did you give her Christmas gifts?" "Did you wear condoms?" "Did she ever drive our cars?"

KEVIN: Wait a minute! Wait a minute!

WENDY: I'm just saying these are things that are going through women's minds and it's real.

KEVIN: Yeah, true.

WENDY: Okay, go ahead.

KEVIN: We went through the question-and-answer thing . . .

WENDY: . . . several times. Because every time . . .

KEVIN: . . . we went through the question-and-answer thing. And we examined it for what it was . . .

WENDY: . . . several times . . .

KEVIN: Aside from all that, I'm not trying to go out and meet nobody else and start this whole shit over again. I wasn't looking for another wife. I honestly think if it's not going to work with me and Wendy, it ain't going to work with nobody. This is it for me. I will be solo and just be by myself. I'm never trying this marriage thing again. I will leave it alone.

WENDY: He said he'd be a lone wolf and ruthless to the chicks if we ever broke up.

KEVIN: Right. Right.

WENDY: And I believe him. According to him I have ruined him for love.

KEVIN: I think it's equal. We realize that aside from this happening we are really good for each other. I had to tell her, "Wendy, you already know a lot of my works. You know the kind of man I am. Of course, cheating is not something any woman should condone. But the way I carry myself, the way I put it down for you. You know. Yes, I did a slimy thing, but it doesn't make me a slimy person. I know I was wrong."

The shit was real rough. And I know it's still a punk-ass way to go out. But at the time, it was what I thought I needed.

WENDY: And even though this was the first time I ever had to experience anything like this, as a smart woman I had to weigh everything. No I wouldn't condone this going on in our relationship again. I would never say, "Yeah, sure do what you want, I'll still be around," because if it happens again, I don't know if that's what I'll do. But Kevin has represented himself in a way where there is no comparison.

KEVIN: Bottom line after all the work we put into this relationship and after everything we've been through together neither one of us wanted to throw it all away. And neither one of us wants to see the other with somebody else. I put a lot of work into her. And she put a lot of work into me. Things got fucked up. Either we're going to rise above it, move on and be stronger or we're not.

We rose above it. We obtained a lot more from having had the experience. And that other person is no longer in the picture. It's just me and Wendy and Junior.

WENDY: And I believe that. And you know what? Kevin can

come in at four o'clock in the morning and I'm not even thinking about where he might have been. I think he's out there
doing exactly what he tells me he's doing—wielding deals for
the benefit of our family. Unfortunately, in this business it
doesn't go down—"it" meaning the power deals—until after
dark. Being a mother, I oftentimes get sent home either via limo
or car service or I drive myself. I want to get home, get some rest
and start my day fresh. I may hear the garage door go up and it
will be five in the morning. And I'm not checking his drawers or
anything.

KEVIN: I could talk to Wendy about pretty much anything now.
That experience helped me realize that she was my best friend.
A lot of dudes feel like the shit they're going through they have
to shield from their lady. After going through that situation I
realized I could talk to her about anything and she can handle
it. We both don't have to worry about hearing that divorce
word.

WENDY: Although he uses it from time to time.

KEVIN: Yeah, I throw it around just to test her game. Her being in
the position she's in and knowing she can pretty much have
any nigga she wants, I want her to know that, "Yes, I know
we're in a special situation, but fuck it, I am willing to leave all
of this and let you do your thing if that's what you want."

Sometimes you have to put that on the table.

Marriage is a partnership. It's a union, it's love. Yeah, you go
in front of the preacher or the justice of the peace and declare
your love. But when you break up you go in front of the lawyer

and the judges, like you're a company or corporation or some shit.

WENDY: And one thing—

KEVIN: Hold up, let me get this thought out.

WENDY: Okay.

KEVIN: When you break up, you say, "Here are your options." Just like dealing with any contract or negotiation. It's good to know you have the option to get out anytime you want. That's why I throw around the D word. I want her to know that I'm not trying to leech off of her or take her for anything.

Her first marriage was fucked up. She got out but she had to go through this process trying to get out of it and keep what she brought into the relationship. On some foul shit.

It took a long time to gain this woman's full trust. I felt that from meeting her in the beginning there were a lot of things that Wendy tried to keep close to the vest, not knowing if she opened up that a nigga might do to her what the last nigga did. It took a long time to get to a point where we are right now. She totally trusts me and I totally trust her. And if she really felt like she wanted out, she never has to worry about me taking a thing. If this fucking lifestyle we're living is bigger than what we have as a couple, take it.

Go find you some nigga who is going to listen to you totally and "Yes, ma'am" you to death.

WENDY: Yeah, like in *How Stella Got Her Groove Back*.

KEVIN: Yeah, it would have hurt me if she took me up on my offer. But I didn't want her to feel like she was stuck with a nigga who is afraid to leave a certain lifestyle. I know I'm a go-getter regardless. Even if I leave with nothing and leave her with everything—including the shit I bought—I know she's still going to have a void there as big as mine. This is all material shit. All of this is expendable. This shit can be here today, gone tomorrow. When that shit went down at HOT-97 and there was a perception that Wendy wasn't on top anymore you could really see who was down for her and who wasn't.

This shit can be here today, gone tomorrow. If you don't have a strong bond, a strong union, none of these things matter. We're bigger than a lot of shit—even a little infidelity, which wasn't the plan. But, yes, we're even bigger than that.

WENDY: It wasn't little. It wasn't little to me and I did a lot of inner soul searching that he knows nothing about to deal with it.

KEVIN: We know about the infidelity . . . can we move on?

WENDY: As far as I'm concerned he got out right before she could stick a pin in a condom or start to want things for Christmas. Women say that they can get down like a dude can and can have sex without emotional attachment.

There are some women who can play that, "Yeah, I'm just like a nigga; I can fuck without emotion." And I think she can . . . for a moment. But eventually we all fold like cheap suits.

KEVIN: Let's rephrase it like this: She made me understand that our working relationship wasn't paramount to going through whatever it was that we were going through. And I proposed to her that if she didn't want to go through it, she could be out. We both realized that that wasn't what we wanted. I love her and she loves me and that's where it is. And that's that.

CHAPTER 14

Big-Body Girl

WENDY WILLIAMS—*five-feet-eight, one hundred and forty-nine pounds.*

Mrs. McCarthy, my sixth-grade gym teacher, announced my height and weight in front of the whole class during health class for a fitness exam. It was one of the more humiliating experiences of my school life. While she weighed everyone and announced everyone's height and weight it seemed as if when she got to mine, time stood still and everyone's ears perked up to hear. I wasn't obese by any stretch, but my weight—which was among the heaviest in my class—caused quite a few snickers and a few wise cracks.

I have struggled with weight my entire life. My first diet was in the first grade. While other kids were bringing peanut butter and jelly or bologna sandwiches from home, I would have a small can of tuna fish (in water, not oil) with mustard (not mayonnaise) in a Tupperware bowl. It was not a sandwich. There was no bread, just tuna and mustard in a bowl. By the second grade my mother got a little generous and added a slice of the Pepperidge Farm wheat bread, the real thin bread. But I only got that once a week. I never had any chips or cookies or anything like that, either. Not a single Ho-Ho, Ring Ding or Yodel.

Every night I would steal change off my father's dresser (he would always empty his pockets when he came in from work) and on my way to the bus stop I would dump out that tuna and mustard and put the Tupperware bowl back in my bag. When it was lunchtime I would buy a hamburger, french fries, the works. This went on for a while until my parents realized that the little diet they had me on was somehow having the opposite affect.

My parents tried everything. After the tuna and mustard diet, there was the Carnation Instant Breakfast diet—Carnation for breakfast and lunch and a sensible dinner, which would consist of a piece of fish or meat the size of the palm of my hand, vegetables and a salad with light dressing. Then there was the broil-everything diet. I could have nothing fried. I was on the Alba 88 diet that was like a milk shake. That worked the same way as the Carnation diet. I had an Alba shake for breakfast and lunch, with the sensible dinner. There was even the no-bread diet where I ate only chef salads.

When none of that worked, my parents resorted to the humiliating Friday morning weigh-ins. When the weight was not coming off, I guess my parents assumed that I was cheating and eating. They were right. I tried everything to get out of the weekly weigh-ins. First, I tried waking up earlier than my parents, getting dressed and going downstairs hoping my readiness for school would thwart the weigh-ins. But it didn't work. They made me get on the scale anyway. Fridays turned into fight days in my house with me protesting the weigh-ins and my parents insisting that I do it.

I finally devised a plan. I learned how to lean on the scale at an angle so that the numbers would go down anywhere from four to eight pounds. I practiced rigging that scale when my parents were at work. The lean had to be just right. I found another trick—putting the scale on the bathroom rug instead of on the hard floor was good for another couple of pounds.

They even tried teasing—albeit good-natured. My brother and sister used to call me "wide-body jet." And my father would say things like, "You're so pretty, if you would just lose some weight." These things were never said in malice. It would always be in the middle of high comedy at the Williams house. My father might jokingly say at dinner, "You might want to put that extra helping of mash potatoes back, Friday's coming."

My mother would never participate in any of the jokes because my weight was not a laughing matter to her. She was very frustrated by my weight. My mother would say, "You know, Wendy, I just bought you those size twelves and now we have to take them back and get a thirteen. What are you going to do next, girl?"

Mothers want their daughters to be in the image of them. Now that I'm a parent myself I understand that. Wanda was the perfect image of my mother, a cotillion queen. I looked nothing like my mother, who was very conscientious about her weight. Both my parents were weight conscious, even to this day. My father is six feet tall and a perfect physical specimen. My mother is five-foot-one with a fat booty (perfect black woman's booty), small breasts and wears a size eight clothes and eight shoe (really a seven but she takes an eight because she had bunion surgery and needs the extra space for comfort—TMI). Their first daughter was a cotillion queen and their second daughter had a weight problem. I know they only wanted the best for me and it was tough on them. But it was tougher on me.

I couldn't even talk to my sister about it because we had absolutely nothing in common. My younger brother had a minor weight problem. But to my parents he was a boy growing into a man's body. Well, I was a girl growing into a woman's body.

My mom would buy my brother Twinkies and count them at night to make sure that I didn't have any. I would try to bribe Tommy to give me a Twinkie. And he usually did. Behind my bed on any given night you could always find candy and Twinkies rappers. But when my brother and I were fighting he would hold the Twinkie caper over my head and run and tell my parents I was eating them.

This weight thing got so bad that by the time I got to high school I was bulimic. Well, I tried to be bulimic. I used to throw up out of my bedroom window. I had to lean out real far so that none of the vomit would hit the house. I tried throwing up in the bathroom but it always made such a mess and I was not trying to ever clean a toilet. So that ended my bout with bulimia.

In addition to sneaking and trying to dodge diets, I had another secret—I wet the bed. I was a bed wetter until I was about twelve. I would wake up in the middle of the night, find my sheets wet, take them off my bed and hide them in the back of my closet. I would put on clean sheets and start the routine over again the next night. And when it got really bad, I had to flip the mattress over.

I might have gotten away with it but the smell must have been too much and Mrs. Johnson, the housekeeper/nanny, found the smelly sheets. I'm sure she told my parents. I kind of wish that I had had a personal relationship with Mrs. Johnson where I could have talked to her and that would have been our little secret. But I didn't. I was too embarrassed.

When my parents found out, I got in trouble and somehow they managed to blame the bed wetting on my weight. "You know your weight is putting pressure on your bladder," my mother would say. She tried to get the doctor to put me on Ritalin for my weight (I have no idea how that would have helped).

I experienced what many young girls are going through today. There is even more pressure today for girls to be thin and perfect. Every little girl wants to be Britney Spears. Little girls, seven and eight years old are looking at Britney and looking at Christina Aguilera and wanting to be that thin. It's an unrealistic image for girls to try to attain. And the magazine covers don't help with these waif-thin models, setting the body-image standards. It's just one more thing to make a girl feel like she doesn't fit in.

But a funny thing happened through all the diets and teasing and humiliation. I learned that size does matter. I learned that I never wanted to be a size six, that I never longed to be small. I learned that being nearly six feet tall and being a big-body girl could come in handy one day. There's power in my size. I can walk into a room dressed in black, in some three-inch heels to make me six-feet-two, with my red lipstick and my "teased and popped" hair and all eyes will be on me.

I don't have to work nearly as hard as the small girls to get noticed. I don't have to take my shirt and specially rip it to expose parts of my body. I don't have to wear embellished, tight jeans with the fringes down the side and all of that. All I need is some red lipstick (I love red lipstick and I love pink), my hair done (I love big hair) and I am the center of attention because of my size.

Big girls need to know it and work it. You will find that your height speaks volumes. You are way more of a presence than Lil' Kim in some pasties. And you are taken more seriously. I don't give a fuck about pasties, pum-pum shorts and all that stuff. You can command just as much attention being tall and strong. Now once you get that attention, big girl, what are you going to do with it? Are you going to take it and do something good with it or are you going to be some dumb trick on a nigga's arm. Me? I'm Wendy Williams. I'm taking it to the top.

Yes, I do know how tough it is growing up. I know what it is to be self-conscious of your height and want to wear flats, hunch your shoulders, and slouch down in your chair. I know what it's like to be at end of the line or taller than every boy in your fifth-grade class. But trust me, if you stand tall, it will eventually work in your favor. Girls with height, be grateful! And make sure when you do walk into a room that you carry your smile with you, too—

especially if you're trying to snag a man. Nothing works better than your presence coupled with a killer smile.

I'm not saying you should walk around just grinning. Know when to use your killer smile. If you don't smile at a brother he will assume that you're taken—which is why I never smile back—or that you're a bitch or maybe even a lesbian. All kinds of assumptions happen when you're an outstanding woman of size—in height with a few pounds on you. I'm not talking about Naomi Campbell tall, who is a six-foot-tall waif model. If you're big-body tall it's so important to plaster a smile on your face.

It's also extremely important that you carry yourself with confidence and that you love who you are. I love myself. Even when I didn't always like things about myself, I have always loved myself—no matter what people around me thought.

I had plastic surgery because I love myself. I loved myself enough to be the best I could be and if that meant fixing something that I didn't feel represented the true me, then I fixed it. If there is a particular aspect of your physical self that you do not like, why suffer with it? Fuck it, get it fixed or change it if you can afford to.

One of the first things I wanted to have done was my breasts. For me it wasn't a matter of being flat chested, which I was a fatty A-cup. Breasts are basically fat and if I were thin I would have been a solid A-cup—on one side. Yes, I was lopsided. My right breast was a fatty A-cup and my left breast was a fatty B-cup. This lopsidedness made me really self-conscious especially when it came time to be intimate with a man. Fortunately, I was never into cheap sex or one-night stands so if I was having sex it was with someone who first got to know me, which lessened the'anxiety. But nobody wants to get involved with someone and have any reservations about taking off their clothes.

Prior to getting plastic surgery my tactic was to slay them with my personality so that when I took off my clothes they would care for me enough not be critical. Fortunately, I have never had any man say anything negative to me about my body. But inside I knew what I wanted—bigger breasts. And you know me, I couldn't just go for the C or the D, I had to do it big, big, big.

I was determined that while I was at it, I would also have liposuction and a tummy tuck. Why stop at the breasts, let's just do the whole damn body. I plotted on plastic surgery since I was young back in Wayside. Among the group of girls that I hung out with the notion of plastic surgery was quite normal. In fact, it was nothing for a girl to get a nose job as a Bas Mitzvah gift. For that community, plastic surgery was not taboo, as it is in the black community. I got comfortable with the idea early.

I also decided that when I got my plastic surgery I would pay for it myself. If this is something you want to do for yourself—and you should only be getting it done for you—then you should pay for it. Don't get it unless you can afford it. And don't finance your plastic surgery. I know I would be pretty pissed if I was still paying for my boobs today. I don't believe you're supposed to finance things like a new body. You finance a house, you finance a car, you don't finance boobs. You're supposed to pay for those muthafuckas cash. And don't ask your boyfriend or your man for the money, either. Do it for you because he'll want them back if you ever break up. At the very least you'll look like a real chickenhead when you break up and he tells the whole world that he bought you your boobs. Save up and pay for your plastic surgery. I put away a little out of each paycheck until I had enough to cover what I wanted to get done.

Another thing I did was *not* discuss my decision with anyone. I didn't tell my girlfriends or my family what I was going to do. I didn't want to hear any nay-saying nor did I want anyone's opinion. I was doing this for me and I didn't expect anyone to understand why. When I got my surgery I blocked out anyone or anything that could possibly scare me. Celebrities don't talk about surgery so you don't get those scare stories or great stories. They simply don't talk about it. I didn't talk about it with my family and I didn't talk about it with my friends so I had nobody from the old school saying, "Wendy, you know what can happen to you?"

The only person I really talked to about what I was going to do was Kevin, who eventually became my husband. In fact, I told him the first night we hung out. I knew I liked him a lot and if he was going to be a part of my life he had to be okay with my decision to get plastic surgery. I needed to know if he was down with it. If he wasn't he had to go. It was that simple. If he was going to have a problem with it, I couldn't be with him because this was something I needed to do for me. And if the man I was with couldn't understand that, bye-bye. Fortunately, Kevin completely understood and supported my decision.

And he didn't say anything like, "Yeah, yeah, get the biggest titties they got!" He was pleased with my original body. He fell in love with that woman. That was a huge plus. I clearly remember my first husband and several of the boyfriends that I had in the past who were dead set against plastic surgery. The funny thing is that it was always the Brooks Brothers men that I dated who never liked a lot of makeup, my red lipstick and the big hair. The Brooks Brothers set never liked any embellishment. They liked me natural. I don't know why, but I knew ultimately that I had to break free and be the woman I always felt I was inside. I knew my outside had to match my inside.

I was glad Kevin willingly supported my decision. I didn't want to be with a man who just went along with what I wanted just because I forced him into it. I'm too strong a woman to want to be the boss at home. I believe the man needs to be the man of the house.

Not only did Kevin support my decision to improve my appearance; he participated. He would treat me to facials and manicures. He would bring home overstated jewelry. He understood the "Bedazzler" inside of me and he fed it. He also understood the business I was in and how important it was to have jewelry and things that make a statement. He knew I couldn't have a simple, understated Cartier watch; I had to have a big, loud, colorful thing with diamonds. When he presented me with my engagement ring, it was a huge diamond surrounded by smaller diamonds. And when he made a little more money he got that ring turned into a necklace, which I still wear today, and gave me an even huger diamond surrounded by big diamonds. He buys me a new fur every winter. Kevin was definitely in on creating the

Wendy people see today. But he was the only one I let in on my plans.

If I told my parents my plans, they would have probably said something like, "Liposuction? Wendy, all you have to do is push back from the table. A good diet and exercise will fix all of that." Who the hell wants to diet and exercise when you can have liposuction? I didn't want to wait. I wanted my new body now.

I got the liposuction first. It was large volume so it had to be done in two sessions. I got my thighs done first and my stomach and boobs next. There was a waiting period of about two months in between the surgeries. The only preparation I made was saving my money. I paid fifteen thousand dollars for the two liposuctions and the implants. And I paid cash.

I found my plastic surgeon through my gynecologist. My first gynecologist did not approve of me getting plastic surgery and kept trying to block and talk me out of it so he got dropped. You either ride with me, or you get out and walk. My new GYN approved of it and was able to give me very good recommendations. I went for a few consultations, compared the results of former patients, talked to women in the waiting area who had had work done and were back for more and settled on a surgeon. I went in, got my surgery and was out of commission for a couple of weeks. I was black and blue. The doctor already told me about the swelling, which would last for about three months. I had to wear compression undergarments for weeks. At the home front I had plenty of big clothes and I had someone to get me my Jell-O. I had someone to confide in and someone who could hold my hand and help me lower myself onto the toilet because the impact of a plop would send my whole body into shock.

One word of advice if you're going to get liposuction or breast implants: Make sure you have someone at home to take care of you. Don't just get plastic surgery and expect to come home to an empty house. I was so grateful to have Kevin.

I didn't just decide I would get the surgery and go in and get it. I researched. I plotted and planned for years and I knew exactly what I was getting myself into. There were no surprises—not the swelling, not the pain, not the bruises. I knew in a couple of months that would all be behind me and it was. I went back and got the boobs and the stomach done.

I booked a flight to Daytona Beach, Florida, two months after everything was done. I was going to my condo, which my parents called home for six of the ten years I owned it. When I arrived, they met me at the airport. I had on a big sweatshirt and baggy pants. I didn't want to hit them with it then. When we got back to the condo, I changed for the pool and when I came out in my two-piece, "wow!" everything was out in the open. I didn't say a word; I let my boobs and the rest of my body tell on me. My parents weren't too shocked. It was a very Wendy thing to do.

I went back to the plastic surgeon after little Kevin was born. After the baby and a hundred pounds, I needed a tummy tuck. So six months after the baby was born, I scheduled the tummy tuck, a little more liposuction on my thighs and I got my implants replaced. Implants should be replaced every ten years because the casing wears thin. So I replaced them early with the same size implant. There are no scars from where the doctor did the lipo-suction. All I have to show for my surgeries is a tiny smile line from one hip bone to the other. And it's fading. While it will not fade completely, I'm fine with it because my stomach is flat.

Getting plastic surgery was one of the best things I have ever done for myself. I have absolutely no regrets. Just because I got liposuction and a tummy tuck doesn't mean I can wild out and eat whatever I want. I still work out and I still try to watch what I eat. The fat won't come back in the areas that had the liposuction but it can turn up in places where you least expect it to. I get it around my face area, so I definitely have to watch my weight. But it's good to be able to go into my closet and throw on whatever I want and not stress about how it will look around my thighs or if the shirt is long enough to cover my stomach. I can now wear midriffs and tight clothes with confidence.

But I still struggle with that fat girl of my youth. Every now and then she rears her ugly little head. When I'm around my parents and my brother and sister sometimes I fall back to being the "wide-body jet" in my head.

Unless you get your issues straight, you're going to gain the weight back. I'm not going to gain it back; like Whitney Houston said, "I will never be fat," because I feel as though I have control over my weight. I will always be a big-body girl in my head and I'm always going to have to watch my weight, but I'm never going to let myself be out of control again.

For one, liposuction regulates where you can gain your weight back. I got virtually every part of my body done except my neck and my upper arms and I'm not trying to have them blow up because they are already big. And my neck? Oh my God, can you imagine that?

Liposuction isn't a permanent cure for being overweight. If you're going to power eat every fucking day like a cow, the fat will eventually grow back around the liposuctioned areas. And imagine how that will look. So you have to control your issues.

I still feel like the awkward girl trapped in big hair and red lipstick every now and then, but for the most part I feel like a great big beautiful doll. And it's more about coming to terms with who I am now as opposed to fighting to get any thinner or fighting to not gain the weight. I love who I am physically now because I have matured emotionally. But that self-acceptance has come hand in hand with getting liposuction. Part of that has given me power to accept myself.

Surgery gave me body acceptance. I say boola-boola to all you women out there who don't care how you look. Boola-boola to women like you and Star Jones. I was never comfortable being overweight. I always felt like a smaller woman trapped in that big body, waiting to be unleashed.

I'm sorry if I'm not like you—accepting yourself as you are. I will not! I want to wear belly shirts and have big boobies and when I sit on top of my man and ride him I don't want to see anything jiggling. But at the same time, I'm still not the perfect-body girl you see in the videos. I'm just perfect for me. And I feel sexy and I feel great.

I know I'm not perfect but plastic surgery has allowed me the freedom mentally to be me. Now I can trip on other things as opposed to tripping over what I'm wearing and whether it is hiding my fat. Now I pop out of bed and I know I can wear anything in my wardrobe. I remember that used to be the biggest battle of the day. What can I put on that's not going to emphasize this or that on me? That used to be the biggest battle of the day. And now that is the least of my worries. And, no, I will not grow old gracefully, dammit! I will grow old mentally gracefully, but I will fight the physical aging the whole way. If I ever see where I need a face-lift, I will get it. If I ever see where I need my eyes done, I will get them done. And it's not about my husband because a man will leave you whether you're beautiful or ugly. It's all about my mental health. It's about me.

Looking back I was never really that fat and damn my parents for making me think I was the largest person in the world. And damn them for creating a woman who in many ways still sees herself as a fat girl. I don't care how much weight you lose or how flat your tummy or thin your waistline, if you've ever been overweight and it's been an issue, you will eternally be a fat girl in your head. You will always be counting calories and looking in the mirror for that bulge of fat.

But in the midst of that you have to know that whatever your size you are beautiful. Whatever you are working with, work it to the fullest. And if you don't like something and can afford to, don't be afraid to change it.

This is not a how-to guide for liposuction or any plastic surgery. I wanted to share my story because too many women, particularly black women, are trapped in this mindset that you have to be "natural." And that's fine but there are some of us that embrace fake and need to know that that's okay, too. Some of us need help. If everything else is easily obtainable—you get your vision corrected if it needs it, your hearing corrected if it needs it, you get your feet fixed if they need it—why shouldn't we fix the things that make us feel better about ourselves? Why can we make a whole turkey dinner in the microwave in five minutes, why can we do our banking on-line, but if you want to lose weight or drop inches through surgery, it's a problem?

People say you shouldn't have liposuction, enhance your breasts or put a hair weave in because that's "fake." That's ludicrous. While the rest of our people (whoever they are) want to be so on this pro-natural kick, how about having natural personality, dammit! So many people walk around being so fake and phony but I keep it real on my radio show and with people. Physically speaking I kept it fake and so what? I'm fake and keeping it real. And I'm telling you how I did it and letting you know you can do it, too.

CHAPTER 15

Advice Hour

I HAVE HAD A LONG-STANDING FEATURE on my radio show called "Advice Hour," and it goes from three until four every afternoon. Now, I'm not a professional shrink or counselor or anything like that. I'm just a woman who has been through some stuff. I don't necessarily think of what I do as giving advice so much as simply putting myself out there as a sounding board for people to bounce things off of. What I tell people is what I would do in the situations they tell me about. In the end, everyone really needs to come to their own conclusions on the things in their own lives.

During "Advice Hour" about ninety percent of the questions I get are about relationships. I get a lot of questions asking me about cheating, like, "Wendy, I found out my man has cheated on me, what should I do?"

Well, before it happened to me, I thought the answer was simple—Leave! I mean, how dare he?! I thought, "Hell, no! I will not put up with a man cheating on me. I'm better than that."

Then it actually did happen to me, and you know what? It's

not the worst thing in the world. And, depending on the circumstances, the act of infidelity might even make you both stronger as a couple. My advice: Yes, you can survive cheating. Not multiple cheats, like cheat after cheat. But a relationship can survive cheating. But, ladies, if he has cheated in a prior marriage or a serious relationship, let that be a warning, a red flag. Because if he cheated on his former woman, especially if it was with you, then it's likely that he will cheat on you, too.

I used to have a "cheat and I'm breaking this shit off" rule, but my husband cheated on me after we got married, not before. Looking back, had he cheated before marriage and before the baby I don't know what I would have done (most likely, broken up with him). Cheating is one of those things where you have to be in the situation to be able to say what you would do. And it has to be your situation, not your girlfriend's situation. She can't necessarily give you advice on something she has not been through firsthand. Now I have modified my rule to: cheating that produces a baby or an STD is a reason to break the shit off.

And I make sure that I keep my shit tight with him, too. I make sure that my behavior is appropriate as well. I have a rule about other men: No hugs or pictures with men. When you hug some men they want to clink you up around the waist and be inappropriate with their hands and that is unacceptable. I don't like it and my husband doesn't like it. And the last thing I want is a picture with another man who is out of line. So, no more pictures with men (who aren't my father, brother, husband—you get the idea).

And now I even have to be careful with women, too. So I had to create a rule about hugging women: No hugging women. I have found there are some lesbians out there (and while I have no problems with lesbians I don't necessarily want to be groped by any) who will be just as inappropriate as some men. And between the lesbians and the Ecstasy pills (which we all know makes some women behave in a manner outside their normal personality) you don't know what angle a woman is coming from. Trust me when I tell you that. I still hug women, but with caution.

I get a lot of questions about dating and how to find a man. And for that question I really have no answers. I have made so many bad choices my damn self in that area and tried too many things before my Kevin came along.

When I was working in Washington, DC, at the oldies station, I used to scan the personal ads. I even had a blind date from one of those phone lines. I believe in that. Even though I was way ahead of my time with that and didn't feel like I needed to do that, I think out of curiosity I made a date from one of those ads. Being a solitary person, I wasn't really out there like that meeting men back then. So that was an easy way for me to meet someone.

One evening I was home alone, flipping through a magazine, and came across this ad. The guy sounded really nice. So I responded. Unbeknownst to me, the guy ended up being white. We met at the local bar. He was a nice, white guy. But it didn't go any further—he just wasn't my type. Not that I have anything against dating outside of my race, but he was like Opie from May-berry. And I'm not dealing with that, black or white. That was my one experience dating from a personal ad.

Women often ask me how I feel about Internet dating and personal ads and all of that. I am for them. In this new day and age where relationships are so hard to come by, and so many people want to be in relationships, I'd go for Internet meetings and I'd go for the personals. But I say do so with caution.

I was very careful. The man I met never knew what I did for a living. He didn't know where I lived. Our meeting was during the day, in a public place where I had no alcohol and I was not high. It was one meeting. We had a nice conversation and a nice meal. And at the end I said, "You know what, you're a nice guy, but I'm not interested in taking this further." And that was that. He was okay with it. There was no drama and we went our separate ways.

But if I was out there and looking, I would definitely go for a personal ad. That is nothing to be embarrassed about. And if you're going on one of these dates, while I do say be cautious, please leave your friends behind. Don't bring them on your date. I say this for two reasons: Friends have a way of blocking or influencing your opinion. You should be wise enough to evaluate this man on your own. If you like him, then introduce him to your friends, but your friends may not like him for no good reason and poison your mind to him from the jump. Give the man a chance and give yourself a chance to really know whether or not this guy is for you. And another reason why you should leave your friends behind is because one of your girlfriends may like the guy for herself and that's a whole other scenario. Friends just get in the way of you having an honest connection. This man could be Mr. Right or Mr. Good Luck. So go on your own, but make sure it's in a safe, crowded place and that you're completely sober.

Once you get the man, how do you keep him? Since I got married, a lot of my listeners want my thoughts on how to keep the fire burning in their relationship. Well, I've taken the liberty to put together a list of things I live by, and here they are:

1. YOU MUST HAVE A DATE ONCE A WEEK

I don't care whether you've been in a relationship for twenty-five years or twenty-five days, having private time with just you and your mate—where you two can let your hair down, look into each other's eyes, talk about neither work-related nor stress-related things and just be into one another—is extremely important for your relationship. You must make time for just the two of you.

A date is different than just being together. When I get home at the end of the day, I usually scrub my makeup off and wipe off my filled-in eyebrows and pull off my hair (because, yes, my hair just pulls off) and I put on one of Kevin's big tee-shirts. I put a scrunchie on my natural hair, which is fourteen inches long and highlighted like my piece but not as full. And then my man and I lay hugged up in the bed together. That, ladies, is not a date. It is coming home at the end of a long day, getting comfortable, and chilling with my man.

On a date, I may still wear the big tee-shirt (because some men think a big tee-shirt is sexy on a woman) or a teddy or a slinky nightie, but I would leave on the hair and makeup. A date can be in your home. And it doesn't have to do with the woman cooking. It has to do with the man being able to see his woman the way another man would see her. You got the picture? It all has to do with the visual, not the taste buds.

On a date, you would put the baby to bed, close the baby's door *and* your bedroom door. And then you set the entire mood for your man. Maybe you take on the characteristics of a cat in bed or something like that. Have you ever observed a cat and how they move very sensually and sexually? Take *that* to the bedroom and see what happens.

Of course your date could take place in a restaurant, but make sure you're fully done up, with your cleavage pumped up. I suggest a dinner at a nice restaurant that has candles on the table so you can hold hands and look longingly into each other's eyes over the natural light.

Whatever you decide to do, make sure you do it once a week, where you are something other than a mother in a dirty throw-up robe or the nine-to-five working woman. Make sure on that day you're "the other woman."

My husband and I do go out at least twice a week for business. I have appearances or I host these big parties. But those aren't our date nights. There is a difference between my party nights with the public and my party nights with Kevin. On his nights, it's all about him and I'm totally paying attention to him. Be sure to mix it up, too, because the same thing every single week won't cut it after a while. Use your imagination.

2. BE THE OTHER WOMAN

I find role playing to be a very important part of keeping a relationship alive. This can be anything from serving him dinner when you normally don't, to calling him baby, to being out to dinner and pretending to be a naughty mistress, rubbing his leg with your foot under the table.

You've heard the expression, "He wants a wife around the house and a whore in the bedroom." This is true. Be his whore. It's not degrading; it's between you and your significant other. He knows who you are and he's not pimping you out—that's why they call it role playing.

You can put on your prescription glasses if you only wear them at night or for driving and become the librarian or the schoolteacher. Curse. Yes, curse during sex, especially if you never curse in real life. Don't be crazy and talk about his momma, but turn on the potty mouth. I find that that is a real turn-on for many men.

So many of us who have been in a relationship for a while get into having routine sex or quickies, but remember to take your time and make it adventurous. Have fun. Be that whore. All men like whores, even if they don't admit it. Being a whore requires you to keep the lipstick on. (I prefer red, but it can be so sloppy, which isn't necessarily a bad thing. Maybe you do the red lipstick the day before the sheets are going to be changed.)

Maybe you wear a wig that you would never wear out of the house or makeup that you would never dream of wearing to your job—whatever it takes, do it. You should come out of yourself and act, act, act. Just be raunchy with it. Let him screw you in the alley next to the club. Let him screw you in the back seat of your car. A lot of these SUVs have a big enough middle compartment where you can barely reach over and slob his knob. But damn you, get it together and reach over and do it, do it, do it!

3. MAINTAIN YOUR ATTRACTIVENESS

Say what you want, ladies, but you looking your best is very important to your man. Beauty is relative, but what got him hooked to you is what attracts him to you. This means your worst day looks-wise must be the day he met you. Period. You have to find ways to look better than the first day he met you. Check out the women he checks out—maybe one of those bitches on the Spice Channel or a chick in a Jay-Z video. Whatever it is that your man likes, you have to be willing to give it to him.

Wear the sexy garments even if they are uncomfortable. Heck, they won't be on very long anyway. You know what my husband seems to really enjoy on me which is so ridiculous because I spend all this money on expensive undergarments? He likes a scrunchie full of hair and a pair of LaPearla underwear, like Jay-Z says. It doesn't necessarily have to be "LaPearla." Maybe it's just a Victoria's Secret thong or something. The point is, don't be afraid to be sexy. It *does* matter how you look.

And, ladies, keep yourselves groomed "down there." Keep your legs shaved if that's what he likes. And ask him, because some men love hairy legs, arms and all that. Find out what *he* likes. And you don't even necessarily have to ask him verbally. Simply pay attention.

I'm a woman who subscribes to maintaining attractiveness regardless of what size I have been. And, surprisingly, my weight fluctuations have never been about men or other women. It has been about me. I know who I've always been in my mind and when I gained a hundred pounds after having the baby I didn't care how many times my husband told me I was beautiful (and he did it very convincingly; my husband made me feel gorgeous), I did not feel like me. When I met my husband I hadn't had any plastic surgery but it was on my mind, and I dressed like a boy to cover up my body. But he always made me feel gorgeous even though I did not feel like the me that I have always envisioned in my mind that I could be. Now I do. Now when he says I'm beautiful, I actually feel it from me, too. When I sense his eyes burning on my backside, I feel like I can buy into it. I can buy into it, because I actually feel it from inside me.

So, maintain your attractiveness not just for him, but mainly for you. Because you're going to find that when you feel attractive you will move more like a cat. No matter what size you are, when you feel good about yourself, you feel like a cat. I'm a size eight in Gap jeans with Lycra in them. When I take off my jeans I have cellulite dimples and all that. But I still feel beautiful. So when he looks at me I feel like his thoughts are secondary to mine. Mine are most paramount. But I feel beautiful and I'm not perfect when I take off my stuff and he knows my boobs are big and fake and he knows that I still feel beautiful. So my third rule is to maintain your attractiveness and never get comfortable because you have been in a relationship for five months or five years.

4. KEEP PICTURES OF FAMILY, FRIENDS AND CHILDREN OUT OF YOUR BEDROOM

There is nothing worse than being hit from the back and opening your eyes and seeing your bunchkin or your mom or your sister on the nightstand smiling at you. Keep the pictures out of the bedroom!

I don't care if you lie in the bed for twenty-eight years trying to have that baby (and believe me, I know the baby means a lot), but take his pictures out of the bedroom or turn them down at least. And your mom could be on the respirator gasping her last breath, but if you're doing the do take her pictures out of your room.

I learned a long time ago to *keep the bedroom romantic*. By romantic, I don't mean all frilly. You're a grown woman and you're having sex. You're not a little girl. If you are a grown woman having a man come over for the night, remember there's not a man out there who will be turned on by teddy bears and unicorns or other stuffed animals lying around your room or on your bed. They will think you have a problem. I'm just giving you a heads up. That unicorn you won at Six Flags when you were nineteen ain't going to win you points in the bedroom. If you're a still a virgin and plan on staying one, then by all means, keep the stuffed animals everywhere. But if you're having sex and you're a grown woman, lose the animals. And I don't care if *he* won the unicorn for you. Put that shit in the closet.

And by the same token your room shouldn't be totally sexed out, either. It's not supposed to be the room of a dominatrix because that is a big turn-off, too—no one wants to feel like they are about to get their ass whipped. If you're in a relationship (and most women are in charge of decorating) be conscious of his masculinity. Don't make the room too pink and feminine. I'm a fan of animal print. Tasteful animal print. And our bedroom is a good mix of masculine and feminine, sexuality and erotica, but not so disgusting that my parents couldn't come in and sit down while I was on bed rest and feel comfortable. Make it sexy, but tasteful. If I had to talk for my husband I would say that he would say, "Wendy is a very tasteful woman." Our bedroom is where it happens, but it is done with taste.

And keep the bills out of the bedroom, too, while you're at it. Keep all signs of bill payment off exposed open surfaces because nobody wants to be reminded about the car insurance or the light bill just before they're about to have their "moment."

5. SPEND TIME APART

My husband and I work together and a lot of time he is even in the studio with me. You guys know that he's my manager and you know he and I are clinked up. We do a lot of business together, but we have our times apart. He has his retail business to take care of and I've got other shit to do besides my four hours on the air.

You just have to spend time apart from your mate. For me that time spent away from him is not spent with my girls because that's not my bag. I have family who live in Miami, Florida, so a lot of my time spent apart from Kevin is visiting my folks in Florida. We're not to the point where I go on girlfriend retreats to Jamaica because that's a bit too questionable and opens the door to all kinds of trouble.

Maybe we can talk about that in another book. On second thought, let's talk about that now.

I don't believe in girlfriends going to Jamaica for the weekend. I just don't think it's appropriate. I mean, what are you doing on a hot, sexy island *without* your man? It leaves too much open for discussion between you and your mate and it's simply not necessary. I believe relationships need rules and boundaries and people need to know what is and isn't off limits. Maybe for you and your man you traipsing off to a hot, sexy island with your girls is cool. But keep in mind if he has no problem with you doing that, you have to give him the same leeway. And what will he be doing while you're gone? I just can't see doing that. Maybe it is because I'm not to that point in my relationship. Whatever. I'm saying it can lead to stuff you just don't need, and I'm standing by it.

My time apart in my relationship can be as simple as the four hours I spend doing the show without him in the studio. And by the time I get home at night separately and by the time he gets home at night separately we say, "How was your day?" and we actually have things to talk about. And since business is intertwined we know exactly who all we are talking about. But it gives us something to share, and that's the point. We spend a lot of time together but time apart is important because if a couple is together all the time they will eventually run out of things to talk about—which means death to any relationship. And I ascribe to the old adages: "Absence makes the heart grow fonder" and "Familiarity breeds contempt."

6. DON'T TALK OUT OF SCHOOL

Don't talk to your girlfriends or anyone else about things going on in your relationship. Once you get in a relationship that you deem serious (and you can tell when that is, whether it leads to marriage or whether the dating leads to living together forever like Goldie Hawn and Kurt Russell), cut off out-of-school talk about your man.

I have found that friends, more often than not, are not the best sounding boards when it comes to serious relationships. Everybody's relationship is different—sure my friend's man might have cheated but her circumstance is different than mine. Sure her man might be in the record industry and go to record industry parties but they don't necessarily roll like we roll. They're just different people, and why they do what they do doesn't have anything to do with me, so their advice can only go so far. Don't even let me get started on the women who give you whack advice only to find out later that they are haters on the down low.

And then there's the chance that your best girlfriend might

talk to her friends about what you told her. The last thing you want is the details of your relationship to be the grist for someone else's mill. It gets around quickly what's going on in your relationship and I had to learn that the hard way. It was a lasting lesson. I haven't had that much backstabbing going on in my life because I was always so cynical and because I followed my own rules from the beginning that I never did run to my girlfriends when things were going wrong in my relationships. This is nothing my mother ever sat me down and told me. It was just something I knew inside not to do.

My most deep conversations that I have with close friends are *after* the problems have mushroomed, been solved and I'm waiting to exhale. Then I'll say, "Girl, you don't understand what I've been through! He did this and this and this." And she'll say, "Wendy, why didn't you call me?"

"Because you know me," I'll say. "I like to sort through my mess and then talk."

You get the point. Don't talk out of school. And that includes to your own family. They can be the worst, because while you may have worked out the problems between you and your man, your family may not so easily forgive and forget. Thanksgiving could be quite uncomfortable after you've decided to take him back and everyone is sitting around the table looking at him, knowing what he did to you. And now everyone is forced to be nice and you have to hope that aunt Wanda doesn't have too much liquor in her and start telling your man off about stuff you squashed months ago.

It puts too much of a strain on the family to involve them in your relationship problems.

You have got to learn that you must be your own best friend and your own best sounding board.

7. PICK YOUR BATTLES

In relationships you have to pick your wars and that means all-out screaming. It's not a battle, it's a *war*. But a war should not be declared because he leaves pubic hair on the shower floor or dirty gym socks in the bed or because he leaves the cap off the toothpaste. Adjust. Figure out a way to get around his minor flaws.

Me, personally, I wash the hair out of the tub, pick up the socks, put the cap back on the toothpaste and keep moving. I don't make it into a big deal. Fortunately, I have always been one for a housekeeper, so a lot of fights other women might have I push off on the housekeeper. I'll just pick up the socks with my big toe and the toe next to it and toss them into the laundry basket. I let the help deal with the rest.

8. BRING YOUR BEST TO A RELATIONSHIP

Always enter a relationship bringing as much to the table as you can. This rule is why I don't believe in marriage before you're twenty-five. You can't possibly bring as much into a relationship at twenty as you can at thirty. In fact, you're not bringing much of anything to the table in your twenties except half-ass credit, maybe a piece of a degree. You have no real job experience or career and no property. You're just a piece of a woman is what you are. You want to build yourself up for you, and bring as much to the relationship as possible because, believe it or not, that will bring out the best in your man. And if he's not quite up to par, he will catch up quickly if he's any kind of man. And if he's already there, that will give him reason to continue.

So always bring something to your relationship. And that includes purity. By purity I don't mean virginity; I mean *no kids*. Yes, how dare I say that? And curse me out if you want but there's nothing like a woman or man coming into a new relationship without kids. It's like starting clean, completely from square one. And in our community finding a mate who doesn't already have kids is so difficult.

I was so amazed when I found my Kevin and he had no kids. He was pure and I was pure. Neither one of us was coming out of a relationship or in one. There was no messy breakup to deal with. It gave us a nice, fresh start where we could concentrate on getting to know one another free from the stress of dealing with kids' "Baby Daddy" or "Baby Mama" drama.

9. KNOW YOUR PLACE

Yes, I know this sounds real old-fashioned but I believe that women should know their place in a relationship. I don't mean that you should be barefoot and pregnant and all of that, or that you should spend all of your time in the kitchen slaving over a hot stove for your man, but respect his space and know you're place.

I don't believe in rifling through a man's wallet or checking his cell phone every night to see who has called. You'd be wasting time and energy and make yourself crazy. You might find something or think you've found something and blow up for nothing. The result would be that you'd look crazy and have put him on the defense. The better way to handle this kind of scenario is to sit back and wait. I am a firm believer that whatever is in the dark will come to light. Just think about it this way. Do you want him going through your purse or checking your cell phone bill? If visions of a possessive stalker come to mind, don't act like one. If something is really going on, trust your gut feelings and wait. It'll all come to light eventually.

Also, I believe very early in a relationship, before it even officially jumps off, you need to establish who does what. In my household we are very old-fashioned. My husband is in charge of the cars. He picks them out; one, because I could give a rat's behind about a car just as long as I look good behind the wheel. But also that's a "man" thing. I don't even care about the color. I just don't want it to be too tricked out. And my husband knows my style and he picks accordingly. He takes care of getting the cars serviced. And he takes out the garbage. And I have the woman's role. I make sure the house is maintained. But if there's a plumbing problem, I call the plumber but my husband gives me the money for him because you know what? Plumbing is a man's job. And I do my woman's work. We are like the secretary of the house. It's my job to empty the dishwasher and load it, wash the clothes, etc. But I don't do that. I make sure it's done. And while I do not exactly cook the meals every day, I make sure everybody eats.

I'm in charge of making sure the house is running, and doing the grocery shopping. He doesn't have to do any of that. I don't even think he knows how much a gallon of milk costs. He decorates the cars, I decorate the house. If I want to throw a pillow there, I throw it there and he better not say anything because the house, that's my area.

We have people who help us, like a nanny, housecleaner, landscaper, cook. But my job is to make the house run smoothly. His job is to make our cars run smoothly. His job ultimately is to make me feel safe and protected. He is the man and that's his primary job. I am the little woman.

10. HAVE A BIG SENSE OF HUMOR

If you really love the big lug, you owe it to yourself to laugh things off. Those lines that form on your forehead from frowning over every little thing you will pay for when they stay there permanently.

If you can laugh, even in the most difficult situations, your relationship will last longer.

CHAPTER 16

Ten Simple Rules

THE FOLLOWING ARE RULES THAT I LIVE BY. They are pretty much self-explanatory and obvious, but I will list them anyway:

1. MAINTAIN A GRATEFUL HEART

You must be grateful for what you have, like your health, your piece of job, your piece of happiness wherever you find it. And maintain a grateful heart every day. You could look at it as a deeper way of saying, "Count your blessings."

2. TELL THE TRUTH

It's okay to tell a lie, but do a "make good" later. If you lie and don't do a "make good," that will follow you for the rest of your life. So you must do a "make good" especially for the purpose of sparing somebody. In the end, though, if you just tell the truth that is what follows you, and there's so much less stress.

While interviewing a guest who has threatened to sue me if I mention his name, he began to talk about my cocaine use and plastic surgery. After getting asked a few tough questions, he thought he could turn the tables on me and suggest that I was still using cocaine and that—not catching a cold from my son—was the reason why I had taken off a few days.

Now this tactic could have worked, if I hadn't followed one simple rule that I have learned over the years—tell the truth. If you come clean and tell on yourself, there's nothing anyone can hold against you. I had talked about my cocaine use and my plastic surgery to my audience until they were practically sick of hearing about it. So when this guest mentioned that I have a cocaine addiction and that's why I had taken off so many days from work, I could say, "Next!" And when he started making comments about my plastic surgery, I could say, "Next!" There was nothing he could say that the audience hadn't already heard. And he couldn't rattle me because not only had I disclosed much of my past, but I was also completely comfortable with where I was. I didn't have any holes that he could poke in and get a reaction.

If you lead your life in an honest and forthright fashion, then no one can come at you about things that you aren't willing to address. Lies and deceit catch up to you.

3. INSIST ON LOYALTY

And give loyalty, whether it's to your friends, to your man or whomever. Don't insist on it and then be a shady motherfucker. Demand loyalty and give it back.

4. TRAVEL LIGHT AND TRAVEL FAR

A perfect example of this: You go to a party and you bring six of your girls with you. If you want to get into the VIP section, it's much easier if it's just you and maybe one other friend. You stand a better chance of getting in than having plus six. Travel light and you could get all the way up into a platinum artist's bed. Or, better yet, all the way up to the top floor of the company. Travel light and travel far applies to everything you do in life.

5. HAVE COURAGE

When things go wrong and your strength is really tested, have the courage to see it through. It's easy to be courageous when everything is going right, but when things are going wrong for you, have courage—it will carry you far.

6. DISCOVER THE POWER OF PRAYER

You don't have to go to church (because I know it doesn't fit into everyone's schedule; some people don't have the wardrobe, and some people don't have a car). Whether you go or not, God is everywhere and He's always there no matter what you're driving. I pray every day, several times a day. And I don't pray for stupid things. I don't waste God's time. He doesn't give a damn if I come out number one in the ratings. I pray for big things—like peace and good health.

7. LOOK FOR THE BEST IN SITUATIONS BUT PREPARE FOR THE WORST

Look for the best, but prepare for the worst. This piece of advice came in handy when I interviewed Whitney Houston. When my husband told me he had secured an interview with her for me through someone in her camp, I was excited, but I prepared for the worst—that she wouldn't come through. Whitney had just been interviewed by Diane Sawyer three weeks prior and was receiving a lot of bad press. She was supposed to call me on a Friday afternoon around four during my show. She was to call from Miami, where she was promoting her album, *Just Whitney*, which wasn't doing too well.

I didn't hold my breath because, quite frankly, during this period Whitney Houston wasn't the most reliable person. And I didn't prepare a single question because if she called during my show, that was *my* time. That was when I would be in my zone and I didn't need any preparation for that. I have been preparing for moments like these for the last fifteen-plus years.

But she did call as scheduled. And from the very first question, I knew we were in for a real show. I thought she might use my show as an opportunity to squelch the criticism she was getting from the Diane Sawyer interview. But she jumped off from the first question by getting in my face verbally and cursing. I knew she would be defensive because I had said things about her in the past on the air that she did not like.

It was one of the most difficult interviews I have ever done and it turned out to be one of the best. In fact, I love a difficult interview where the guest is defensive or nasty because that means the audience will get a treat.

I expected Whitney to be cursing and name calling and carrying on. I prepared for that. Instead of doing my normal scintillating live interview, I taped it—something I never do. When a guest doesn't want to continue with an interview they usually will start cursing. They know that on the radio that's a big no-no and cursing will usually result in the end of the interview. But by taping it (unbeknownst to her), I was able to have my engineer edit all of that out without ending the interview, and we were able to play it the next day in all its glory.

So while expecting the worst I was prepared to give my best, and people are still talking about that interview I had with Whitney Houston.

When you're going into a job interview and you would love to get the job because you're way behind in your bills, prepare for the worst if you don't get it. Make a plan for what you will do if you don't get that job.

Or if you're going for a Pap smear, prepare for the worst—cancer. Make sure your life insurance is in place because it's hard to get once you are sick.

When your man goes out at night, prepare for the worst. What if he doesn't come home? Are you ready?

8. ALWAYS HAVE YOUR "FUCK YOU!" MONEY

I think that speaks for itself. "Fuck you! I don't need this job anyway!" And then you leave. You better make sure you have enough to carry you through, though. If you don't? Well, you better hold your tongue on the "Fuck you!" If you can't afford to say "Fuck you!" then hold your tongue until you can. "Fuck you!" requires at least six months of living expenses—depending on your lifestyle and what's important to you.

And "Fuck you!" isn't just about a job. If you're having a bad date and you want to say, "Fuck you, nigga!" you better have cab fare to get home. That cab money might be a hundred and seventy-five dollars because your first date was in Philly and you live in the Bronx. Make sure you have it . . . just in case.

9. THE ANSWER IS WITHIN

The answer is not with your girlfriends, and it's not in the "Advice Hour" of the *Wendy Williams Experience*. The answer is within you. And if you don't find the answer there, well, you got some work to do on yourself.

10. DON'T DWELL ON THE PAST

You must use the past as a learning springboard to the future. If you stay stuck on the past and continue to dwell on it, it will fill your future.